*
*
*

Life in the Crystal Palace

*
*
*
*
*

LIFE IN THE
CRYSTAL PALACE

*

*

*

*

by Alan Harrington

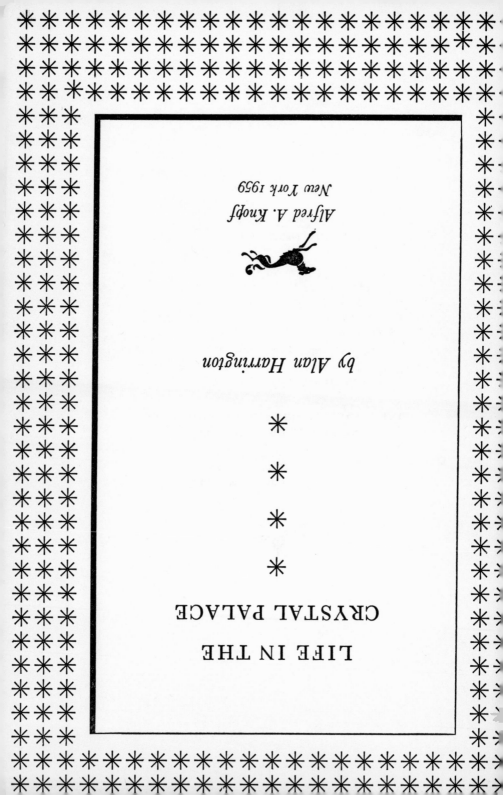

Alfred A. Knopf
New York 1959

L. C. Catalog card number 59–10481
© Alan Harrington, 1959

THIS IS A BORZOI BOOK
PUBLISHED BY ALFRED A. KNOPF, INC.

PUBLISHED OCTOBER 21, 1959
SECOND PRINTING, NOVEMBER 1959

Portions of this work have previously appeared in
The Atlantic Monthly, Esquire, and The Nation.

You believe, do you not, in a crystal palace which shall be forever unbreakable—in an edifice, that is to say, at which no one shall be able to put out his tongue, or in any other way to mock? Now, for the very reason that it must be made of crystal, and forever unbreakable, and one whereat no one shall put out his tongue, I should fight shy of such a building.

Fyodor Dostoevsky
Notes from Underground

This book was written with the aid of a grant from the Fund for the Republic, Inc. The foundation assumed no obligation to pass on or approve the manuscript, and the author was free to write as he pleased. I would like to express my appreciation to the Fund for the Republic and particularly to Mr. W. H. Ferry, vice-president of the Fund, for his interest and confidence in the work that was under way.

Contents

✳

Contents

✳

Life in the Crystal Palace

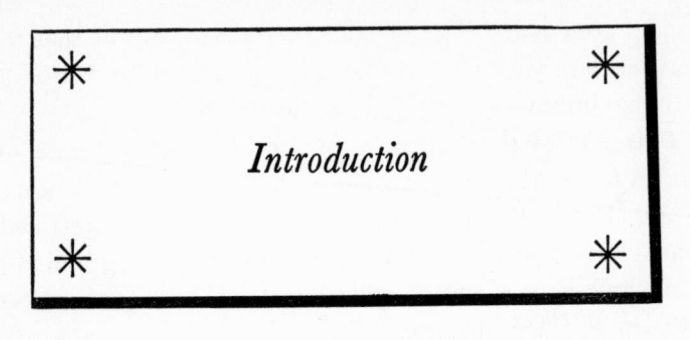

Introduction

The Crystal Palace is one of America's great corporations. We who earn a living in such companies have been characterized variously as corporation men, organization men and women, and (inaccurately) as wearers of charcoal-gray suits. For some years now we have been living under glass. Through our transparent walls observers have been peering, as they would into an ant palace, to discover what in the world animates this strange new being, the corporation person.

I don't blame them for studying us. From the outside looking in we must appear to be a rather peculiar bunch of people. Is it true that we are collectively different from our fellow countrymen? Are we in our corporate glass houses separated from the life going on outside our walls? Not being a sociologist, I can't say with authority whether corporation life has produced a new species of American. But from my own experience at our company I feel that it has.

I think that our new species may be distinguished from other American working people at least in one way, by an absence of nervousness. We are not worried about our jobs, about the future, about . . . much of anything. This is a curious sensation, not to have any real worries. Try to imagine it. How are you going to get ahead? The company will decide. *Quo vadis?* The company will take care of that too. Furthermore your affairs will be ordered fairly and squarely with maximum sympathy for your well-being.

This sort of good-fortune cannot help but separate our species from others who are not so lucky. We are like a man in an electrically-cooled suit, or in winter an electrically-heated suit, wondering why others are perspiring and shivering and why they are running about and jostling each other in animated dispute.

Our protected man is a good person. He faces the world with all-purpose amiability. Assail his position and he will readily agree that you have a point. Swing your fists at the company itself and the answer to your primitive behavior will come in the form of courteous public relations. But how unreasonable to attack him! He is polite, decent and cooperative, and eager to be a good citizen. Besides, your assault will be unfair. *He* is not responsible for the policies that govern his life. No one is. These policies have been formed over the years by ten thousand committees. Like this nice man or not, with each passing year you see more of him. Ask, if you will, whether our founding fathers would draw back in dismay or whether they would be pleased to have the future of the United States entrusted to his care.

As the great companies and their subsidiaries have extended their operations across the country and overseas, hundreds of private enclaves have come into being. (Indeed in some instances they resemble private company-states, insofar as employees hardly exist outside of them.) Mark these enclaves as small circles on the map and you will see the number of circles from Maine to California increasing every year. I am reporting from one such enclave, not as an expert but as an insider looking out. The writer is knocking on the picture window trying to get attention. He is saying: "Here, look. This is the way we live and how we feel about it."

Several chapters of the book go beyond the confines of the Crystal Palace. They deal with what it takes to succeed . . . and to fail, and explore the nervous territory between success and failure. For many decades, I think, we have all been handed the assignment of making good or of suffering, to some degree, humiliation. That has been the law of the business culture that surrounds us. Now the corporation offers relief from that assignment. To give a fair picture of corporation life, I have contrasted what we have with some earlier personal experiences—the excitements and miseries that come with unprotected, unguided living.

I. *Life in the Crystal Palace*

Happy families are all alike, said Tolstoy. Whether this is true of great corporations I don't know, because I have belonged to only one. The company I have been with for more than three years is one of the world's largest, having some thirty-four thousand employees in the United States and overseas. There are more than five hundred of us here at headquarters—and we are a happy family. I say this without irony, not for the reason that I am in the public-relations department, but because it is the truth. We give every appearance of happiness. We are also in many respects pretty much alike, at least on the surface.

It is not that our company makes us behave in a certain way. That kind of thing is out of date. Most of our people tend to live and talk alike, and think along the same general lines, for the simple reason that the company treats us so well. Life is good, life is gentle. Barring a deep depression or war, we need never worry about money again. We will never have to go job-hunting again. We may get ahead at different speeds, and some will climb a bit higher than others, but whatever happens the future is as secure as it can be. And the test is not arduous. Unless for some obscure reason we choose to escape back into your anxious world (where the competition is so hard and pitiless and your ego is constantly under attack) we will each enjoy a comfortable journey to what our house organ calls "green pastures," which is, of course, retirement.

"Is this sort of existence worth living?" you ask. I think that depends on who you are and also on the person you could become. There are two ways of looking at it: (1) If you are not going to set the world on fire anyway, it is better to spend your life in nice surroundings; (2) looking back, you *might* have had a more adventuresome time and struggled harder to make your mark in the world if the big company hadn't made things soft for you.

But it is all too easy to be glib in disapproving of the kindly corporation. We are then in the position of scorning the earthly paradise, and that cannot be done lightly. To be honest, we should put aside the convenient clichés—that big business firms, for example, are by their very nature heartless, exploitive, enforcers of conformity, etc. It is commonly assumed that a big, apparently impersonal authority is made up of bad fellows. How much more bewildering and exasperating to discover that they are good fellows!

I went into my job at the corporation with a poor spirit. I was suspicious of large companies, and swore that nobody was going to turn me into a robot. My situation was untenable anyway. I had just sold my first novel, a satire about a man who, under the pressure of business, had turned himself into a Nothing. In a year the grenade would go off, and of course the writer would be fired.

Particularly disconcerting in the early days was the gentleness of my new associates. Most public-relations offices are filled with edgy, hustling people. Here there was such courtesy and regard for your comfort . . . it was unfair. When I arrived, everyone turned and smiled, and they all came over to say how glad they were that I was with them. The boss took my arm and had me in for a long talk. "We want you to be happy here," he said earnestly. "Is there anything we can do? Please let us know." When you discover that the members of the company team really care about you it is a shock to the nervous system. The skeptical newcomer stands there, shifting his feet, not knowing what to do with his preconceived resentment.

I went through the orientation course, and completed all the forms and saw that I was protected against everything. I had a momentary fearful sensation of being enfolded in the wings of the corporation and borne aloft. "How's everything going?" inquired one of the orientation men, and I grunted at his civil question.

Now I was one of the group, hunched gloomily over a typewriter amid smiling faces. With the exception of the department head and assistant manager, our public-relations staff worked in one large room. We did our jobs in leisurely fashion with a carpet of non-glare fluorescent lighting above and a thick wall-to-wall carpet below. The usual office noises were hushed. Typewriters made a faint clack. Our mild jokes were lost in the air. It seemed to me a strange pressure chamber in which there was no pressure. This was a temporary arrangement. Next year the company was moving to a new office building in the suburbs, and it would be a fabulous place—a great office-palace on a hilltop surrounded by fields and woodlands. Everybody talked about the palace and what a marvelous headquarters it would be. The enthusiasm bored me, and I thought: "Well, I'll never see it."

That was a long time ago. Today I continue to live in the city but commute in reverse to the suburbs, and every weekday I sit down to work in the country palace. Here, after three years, are some general impressions of our corporate life:

The corporation is decent. Most of our men have deep, comfortable voices. You have stood beside them in slow elevators, and heard these vibrant tones of people whose throats are utterly relaxed. And why shouldn't they be relaxed? Once you join our company, so far as the job is concerned, you will have to create your own anxieties. The company won't provide any for you.

There is no getting around it—our working conditions are sensational. The lower and middle echelons arrive at nine and, except in very rare instances, go home at quarter-to-five. Many of the higher executives work longer and harder, according to their inclinations, but seldom in response to an emergency. Rather it is a pleasure for them.

This is a company whose products move easily in great packages across the continent. Demand is constant and growing, since our products are good for people and contribute to the nation's health and well-being. The supply is adjusted from time to time in order to keep prices at a reasonable level. There is no reason for anyone to kill himself through overwork.

The savage, messianic executive of the type described in Rod Serling's *Patterns* would find himself out of place here. In fact, he would be embarrassing. In the unlikely event of his coming with us, the moment he started shouting at anybody he would be taken aside and admonished in a nice way. (We do have one high-ranking officer a bit like that, but he is old and close to retirement. He is very much the exception.)

A full recital of our employee benefits would—and does, in the indoctrination period—take all day, but here are just a few of them. We have a fine pension fund, a fantastically inexpensive medical program for you and your family, and a low-premium life-insurance policy for double your salary. The company will invest five per cent of your pay in blue-chip stocks and contribute on your behalf another three per cent. The company picks up half of your luncheon check. When we moved to the suburbs, the company paid its employees' moving expenses and helped them settle in their new homes. For those who didn't wish to move . . . a bus waits at the railroad station for commuters from the city and drives them to the hilltop office building.

The only unsatisfactory working condition, I think, is that you must be content with a two-week vacation until you have been with the company for ten years. In other words, the experience you may have gained elsewhere, precisely the experience the company has *bought,* counts for nothing in terms of vacation time. But this policy is fairly standard practice. It certainly inhibits a man's desire (say, after nine years) to change companies for a better job. Thus, it is at least a minor pressure against free-spirited enterprise. All the benefits exert pressure, too. There is nothing sinister about them, since admittedly they are for your own material comfort—and isn't that supposed to be one of the goals of mankind? What happens is that, as the years go by, the temptation to strike out on your own or take another job becomes less and less. Gradually you become accustomed to the Utopian drift. Soon another inhibition may make you even more amenable. If you have been in easy circumstances for a number of years, you feel that you are out of shape. Even in younger men the hard muscle of ambition tends to go slack, and you hesitate to take a chance in the jungle again.

On top of all this, it is practically impossible to be fired.

Unless you drink to alcoholism or someone finds your hand in the cash box, the company can afford to keep you around indefinitely. Occasionally under great provocation—such as a scandal that reaches the tabloids—there may be a transfer. Once in a while a prematurely crusty old-timer is retired. Otherwise the ax will not fall.

Every so often I hear my seniors at the corporation inveigh against socialism, and it seems strange. I think that our company resembles nothing so much as a private socialist system. We are taken care of from our children's cradles to our own graves. We move with carefully graduated rank, station, and salary through the decades. By what marvelous process of self-deception do we consider our individual enterprise to be private? The truth is that we work communally. In our daily work most of us have not made an important decision in years, except in consultation with others.

Good people work here. Since joining the company I have not heard one person raise his voice to another in anger, and rarely even in irritation. Apparently when you remove fear from a man's life you also remove his stinger. Since there is no severe competition within our shop, we are serene. We do compete mildly perhaps, by trying to achieve good marks in the hope that our department head will recommend a promotion or an increase to the Salary Committee. Cutting out the other fellow and using tricks to make him look bad is hardly ever done. At higher levels, now and then, executive empires will bump into each other and there will be skirmishes along the border. But these are for the most part carried on without bullying and table-pounding, and the worst that can happen to the loser is that he will be moved sideways into a smaller empire.

It would be wrong to say that our employees are not lively. They smoke and drink and love, and go on camping trips, go skiing, and operate power boats, and read things and go to the movies, and ride motorcycles like anybody else. In the office they know what to do (usually after consultation) in almost any circumstance. What a great many of them have lost, it seems to me, is temperament, in the sense of mettle. We speak of a mettlesome horse. Well, these are not mettlesome people. They lack, perhaps, the capacity to be mean and ornery when the ego is threatened—because at our company we do not threaten people's egos. Rather the ego tends to atrophy through disuse.

Another curious thing is our talent for being extremely friendly without saying anything to each other. I remember a conversation that went something like this:

"Jim! Where did you come from? I haven't seen you in— I guess it's been about a year and a half."

"Just about that, Bill. A year and a half at least."

"What are you up to, for goodness' sake?"

"I've been in Washington, and now I'm going back overseas."

"Always on the move!"

"Well, I guess I am. I just thought I'd come down and have a chat with you before leaving."

"It's great that you did. How's your family?"

"Fine, Bill, how is yours?"

"They're fine, too."

"The years go by, don't they?"

"They sure do."

"Well. . . ."

"Well. . . ."

"Well, I guess I'd better be moving along."

"It's been wonderful talking to you, Jim. Look, before you get on the plane, why don't you come down for another talk?"

"I will, boy. You can count on it."

Also common among our employees is a genuine and lively interest in the careers of upper-level executives whom they may never have laid eyes on. As the gentlemen move from one station to another, their progress is followed with exclamations and inside comments. "Hmm, Jackson has moved to Purchasing! I thought so." "Look at Welsh—he's taken over the top spot in Patagonia. Anybody can tell that they're setting him up for a vice-presidency." Who *cared* about Jackson and Welsh? At one point, I did. I had to prepare a press release about them, and update—add two more lines to—their official biographies.

The role of the corporation's top directors in our cosmos is an interesting one. In our company, members of the board are not remote figures from outside who drop in to attend meetings now and then. They are on the job every day. They recognize us, nod, and often say hello. I have found these august gentlemen to be amiable and even shy in the presence of their inferiors, but their appearance on the scene is the occasion of total respect, body and soul, such as I have never witnessed outside the army. They are not feared either. They conduct themselves in a friendly, most democratic manner. It is not awe they inspire but, so far as I can see, pure admiration. I was once talking to a young man in the employee-relations department when his eyes, gazing over my shoulder, suddenly lit up with joy. I turned, expecting to see our pretty receptionist, but it was a director passing by and giving us a wave of his hand.

Team play is the thing. Team play means that you alone can't get too far out ahead of the troops. You can't, because in our company it is necessary to consult and check over everything. Someone will ask whether this doesn't lead to a certain amount of mediocrity. It does. We have a substantial number of mediocre people in the company—that is, men and women of ordinary ability who would probably never originate anything under any circumstances.

But where organizing an effort is concerned it is sometimes better to have mediocre talent than a bunch of creative individuals who disturb the situation by questioning everything. In terms of performance, if you have a slow but sure operation, mediocre personnel, including your nephews, can carry it out beautifully. In *planning*, mediocrity has and still does hurt the company.

Our method is to get together and talk it out, each one of us contributing his mite. Why have one man make a decision when thirty-three can do it better? The consequence of this policy is that our executives commit few errors—although sometimes they arrive at the right decision three years too late. But the sure markets for the company's products bring in so much money that the mistake is buried under mountains of dollar bills. Our interminable round of conferences may also be counted on to produce by default serious errors of omission. These don't hurt noticeably either, for the reason cited above.

I got over my impatience at the slow pace of things, but I felt it once at a lecture given to senior and junior executives on the new central filing system that would go into effect when we reached the palace. A fierce little girl, a vestal of the files, told us how it was going to be. We sat, without anyone suggesting it, according to rank, and I could work out the possible course of my company career, if I stayed with it, just by looking at the assemblage of heads in front of me—bald and white in the front rows, then pepper-and-salt, and gradually back where I was, the black, brown, and blond heads of hair. I thought of my own head, slowly changing through the years as I moved up a row or two, with never a chance by a brilliant coup of jumping while still brown-headed—or even pepper-and-salt—over several rows and landing among the white thatches. How could I make such a leap when anything I accomplish I do as a member of a group?

A little more tension would be welcome. This may be based on fragmentary evidence, but I suspect that when people are not placed under at least a minimum of tension they seek it out in their dreams. One day I overheard our press-relations man conferring with our public-relations manager, Mac Tyler, who said: "Maybe next time, Walt, you had better try it the other way." The press man came out of the office and saw me. "Boy!" he said, "I sure got a bawling out on that!"

Another man of some rank joined his local Democratic Party, and worked hard at it during the presidential campaign. But he felt guilty about what he had done. Finally he rushed upstairs and confessed to the president of the corporation. "Gosh," he told me afterward in a disappointed tone, "he didn't mind at all. He just put his hand on my shoulder and said: 'Don't worry, Fred, I'm a Jeffersonian Republican myself!' "

We conform by choice. Critics of big business are constantly on the watch for the kind of over-cooperation that a company explicitly demands of its members. Our company doesn't demand anything. Oh, there is tactful pressure on us to join the annuity and insurance program, and a rather strong insistence on Red Cross and Community Chest contributions, but nothing serious.

What you have to watch out for is the amount of compliance you fall into by yourself, without realizing it. Something like this almost happened to me when my book was published. Far from resenting the satire, most of our employees who read it enjoyed the book. I was asked to autograph dozens of copies, and several were bought and prominently displayed in the company lending library. I had thought of myself as a writer in temporary captivity. Now that was no longer possible. A captive of what? Good Will?

I began to feel what I now recognize was a gradually deepening contentment. If you are on the watch for the symptoms, here are a few: (1) You find that you are planning your life defensively, in terms of savings plans and pensions, rather than thinking speculatively of moving up fast—faster than the others. (2) You become much less impatient over inefficiency, shrug your shoulders and accept it as the way things are. (3) Your critical faculties become dull; you accept second-best; it seems unsporting to complain. (4) Nothing makes you nervous. (5) You find that you are content to talk to people without saying anything. (6) You mention something like (improvising now) "our Human Development Department" to outsiders and learn with surprise that they think you have made a joke.

During this period of contentment, which lasted quite a few months, I did not concern myself with anything beyond the requirements of my job. I became easy-going and promiscuously nice, and had a harmless word for everybody. Finally, I was reminded that this sort of thing was the mark of a fat soul. A succession of incidents helped indicate what was wrong.

We are remote from the lives of others. Shortly before we moved to the country the press-relations man and I were looking out of our eleventh-floor window in the direction of the waterfront. We saw a half-circle of men gathered on a far-off pier. "Isn't that what they call a shape-up?" he asked with faint curiosity. It was easy to tell that he barely imagined that these men existed and that their quaint customs were real.

Some weeks before, I had looked down on a gentleman in a homburg and cutaway, running among the crowds in the financial district. He carried a bouquet of red roses wrapped in green paper. You don't associate this street with flowers, and it was exciting to see him running, holding his green wrapping like a torch of something beautiful in this place. And then he died on his feet, twisting over and slumping to the pavement. His head rested against the wall of a building. He rested with the flowers flung across his knees and his fine hat askew, and the absurd and living gallantry that produced this death *could* only be nothing to us or to anyone in the crowds that simply swerved around him and kept going, because of the way we are concentrated and oriented away from things like that.

How remote we were too from the crazy musicians who arrived on a blustery fall day with the idea that, since this was a financial center, there would be a rain of coins from the tall buildings in response to their trumpet, guitar, and bass fiddle. The wind swirled their jazz among the canyons. I saw that no one was paying them the slightest attention. Feeling guilty, I threw them a quarter, but they didn't see it. They danced and made jazz in the cold, while upstairs we went on with our work, and they didn't exist, and it was nobody's fault.

It isn't that we should have been expected to know about longshoremen, or care particularly about the man in the homburg, or throw coins to the brave musicians, but we have simply, systematically, avoided letting these aspects of life into our field of vision. We came in from the suburbs and plundered the city, and left each night without having the least idea of what was going on there. Even our daily experience in the rapid transit was spent behind a newspaper; taxis shielded us from the bad sections of town. We never heard guitars strumming on the dirty doorsteps, nor comprehended the possible excitement of disorderly feelings that make other people so much more alive than we are.

And when the corporation moved to the country our isolation from all that became completely splendid. Now most of us could anticipate fifteen- and thirty-minute rides in car pools from our suburban homes to a suburban office. You could almost hear an official sigh of contentment on the day that we moved.

This way to the palace. Point your car along a winding drive-way up the green hillside shaded with great elm trees. Enter the wide and friendly doorway and look at the murals in our lobby. They will tell you the story of our industry. As you go through the offices, you will probably marvel as we did at all the comforts and services we have. Imagine a sea of blond desks with tan chairs, outdoor lighting pouring in everywhere, roomy offices with individually-controlled air-conditioning and area-controlled Music by Muzak coming out of the walls. We need few private secretaries. All we have to do is pick up a phoning device and dictate our message to a disc that whirls in a sunny room in another part of the building. Here a pool of stenographers type all day long with buttons in their ears. We don't see them and they don't see us, but they know our voices.

A high-speed pneumatic tube system winds through the entire building. We send material from one office to another not by messenger but by torpedo containers traveling twenty-five feet a second. Simply have the attendant put your paper, magazine, or memo in the plastic carrier. He inserts the container in the tube, dials the appropriate number, and, whoosh, it is shot across the building. There is a complete sound system throughout headquarters. If, for example, a bad storm is forecast, there will be an "Attention Please," and you may go home early. At noon, enjoy movies in an auditorium the size of a small theater, visit the library, watch the World Series on color TV, or play darts and table tennis in the game room. The finest catering service and a staff of friendly waitresses bring you luncheon. Then go to the company store, pitch horseshoes, or take a brief stroll under the elms.

What happens to a office force when it is offered facilities like these? At first there were a few small complaints. The main difficulty is that we find it all but impossible to get off the campus. You can speed several miles to town for a quick lunch. Otherwise you stay on the grounds until closing. City employees everywhere have the chance to renew, at least slightly, their connection with the world during lunch hour. When we first came many of us rambled in the woods and picked flowers, but we seldom do that anymore.

As for our work-efficiency, I think it has diminished a bit as a result of what one of my friends calls "our incestuous situation." When you are isolated in the country it is not easy to feel that sense of urgency that distinguishes most businessmen.

I sometimes have a feeling of being in limbo. More than ever one feels—ungratefully—over-protected. While on the job, I actually can't feel hot or cold. I can't even get sick. This will sound ridiculous, but when the company obtained a supply of influenza shots, I found myself in the absurd position of refusing one. For some reason I wanted a chance to resist the flu in my own way.

What is the moral of all this? I am not quite sure, but some time ago Dostoevsky put it in *Notes from Underground:*

"Does not man, perhaps, love something besides well-being? Perhaps he is just as fond of suffering? Perhaps suffering is just as great a benefit to him as well-being?

•　　•　　•

". . . In the 'Crystal Palace' (suffering) is unthinkable.
. . . You believe, do you not, in a crystal palace which
shall be forever unbreakable—in an edifice, that is to
say, at which no one shall be able to put out his tongue,
or in any other way to mock? Now, for the very reason
that it must be made of crystal, and forever unbreakable, and one whereat no one shall put out his tongue, I
should fight shy of such a building."

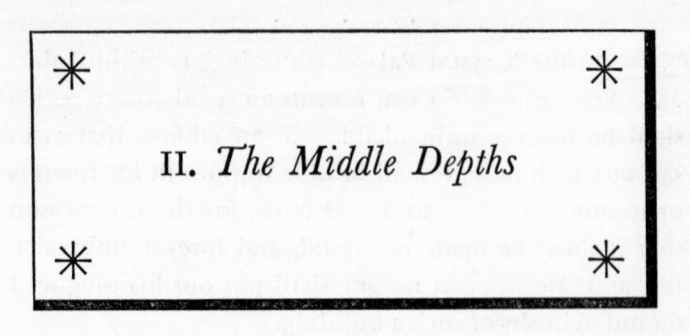

II. *The Middle Depths*

We at the Crystal Palace are not born lotos-eaters; rather, like the members of Ulysses's crew, we have been cast up on this corporate island without any idea of the sweetly powerful effect the lotos will have on our natures. We discover at once that "there is sweet music here that softer falls than petals from blown roses on the grass." This is the music not only of Muzak but of beguiling security. At indoctrination sessions the annuity and insurance people come forward and explain to the newcomers all the benefits that are in store for them. What happened to Ulysses and his men, in Tennyson's lines, now happens to us.

> *"Branches they bore of that enchanted stem,*
> *Laden with flower and fruit, whereof they gave*
> *To each, but whoso did receive of them,*
> *And taste, to him the gushing of the wave*
> *Far far away did seem to mourn and rave*
> *On alien shores. . . ."*

Time goes by, and the once-astonishing benefits become a matter of course. We wonder how we could ever have done without them. A year later we tremble at the thought of doing without them. Twelve months after that the idea is simply unthinkable. The rough waves of fortune and risk are no more than a memory; we listen only to a gentle lapping on the beach.

There arrives a day when the corporate sanctuary becomes our whole world. We can't imagine existing outside of it. From our safe place we watch others struggling amid uncertain currents, and thank our stars and the lucky winds that brought us here. I wake up one morning, and all at once I know that I will never again dare (or care) to be a mariner. I will not venture forth from our haven, nor will you. We look at each other and smile faintly, and say a cheerful good-morning. We go on about our well-ordered business, and we are not the same men and women that we used to be. Not that we are necessarily any the worse for that. On the contrary, many of us are better citizens, better husbands and neighbors, more cooperative and humane than we would otherwise be—if we were subjected to the pressure of a nervous world.

Who are we? What kind of person joins a Crystal Palace? The answer is not "all kinds." The voyagers who arrive at our sanctuary are thoroughly tested, and the unwanted ones given a friendly handshake and thrown back into the ocean. Generally, if you are accepted for a higher-level position at our palace you will be Protestant. On all levels, with exceptions, it is better if possible to be Christian. With these considerations out of the way, you will be taken over an obstacle course of department heads and personnel apprentices, and passed through screens and personality filters developed by industrial psychologists and their apprentices who tap you all over with little rubber hammers.

These preliminaries make it likely, although the system misses now and then, that your friends in the company will be the right sort—with backgrounds and education roughly similar to yours. At this stage of the game there is no corporate type; that comes later. You Do It Yourself. The screening reduces the *range* of men and women you will find at the Palace. Even so, within the confines of our eligibility we can show you minor geniuses and clowns; hidden artistic temperaments; bold and forthright executives; cowards; bright, pretty and sensitive girls; a few oafs and hard drinkers; along with a horde of nephews, clods, and mediocrities . . . with most of these characteristics muted and dulled, yes, or buried alive but still alive, after years of security and soft music.

Alive but not kicking; that is the trouble. What we lose first of all is the divine impatience that built, among other things, the U.S.A. I mean the hustling, abrasive turn of mind that tells you, when some laggard functionary slows up progress: "Throw him out!" Or when the official handbook gets in your way: "Tear it up!" Baseball created the relief pitcher, and when the starter falters we cry from the stands: "Get him out of there!" The same spirit prompted Jim Thorpe to say to his team-mates when all else had failed: "Just give me the ball and follow me!"

As soon as we reach the Crystal Palace we learn that the impatience of traditional enterprise has been almost completely abandoned. Seniority rules, as much as or more than in the army. You are not going to get anybody out of there until he arrives at a certain age. All business must be done by the book, through channels and committees. This can be bewildering to the newcomer, particularly if he is full of bounce and ambition.

It is not that our system is foolish or especially inefficient. If that were true, the company would long since have gone bankrupt. Also we must not forget that in their cumbersome way our committees eventually come up with million-dollar decisions that make economic history. But here I am talking not about the system's economic effects so much as its impact on us, on the employees who live by it, and with it. How to nail down what seems wrong? Conceivably the procedures we have developed are too orderly and, in a remote way, too humane. In an atmosphere of over-all humaneness it is possible for rough, instinctive humanity to dry up.

Who deep down in his heart remains content to spend his working life as an obscure member of a team? Only, it may be supposed, someone without talent. From childhood we call out: "Look at me!" not "Look at us!" The ego gives off sparks. The most natural desire in the world is to want to call attention to yourself, to shine in some respect above the others, to shine *your light* so that it will be noticed. To accomplish that, you make yourself worthy, study, drive, let everyone know you are there, and aim to move ahead quickly.

The Crystal Palace serves, among its many functions, as a protective league for small talents. Within our ranks, no matter how alert you are, the likelihood is that you will wait your proper turn. You can't grab the ball and run with it; the huddle insists on running with you. You are one of the team, will always respond to its signals, and hardly ever call a signal of your own.

This puts the energetic young man in a bind. Embracing him is a kindly, frustrating organization that asks of him but one concession—that he rein in his impulses to run free. Should temptation urge him to take a chance and break away, he hesitates, turning his eyes to the cluster of benefits that will deliver him forever from want and fear.

For our young girls the choice seems easier. "After all," says Nancy Ireland, "it's a job, and it's nice out here." Yes, and any month she will meet the right boy, and the money she has put away under the savings plan will be like a dowry. Often things will turn out that way. But we will see another girl for whom the time goes by without a boy. Having moved to a suburb near the Crystal Palace, she shares an apartment with a girl or two. There are not so many young men around here. Meanwhile the mound of savings grows steadily larger. She begins to identify her safety with the job at the Palace. Outside affairs become less real. The cheerful office life extends to after-hours. She may be found more and more at company social outings, and takes to traveling in a pack of company girls for bridge, picnics, and desperation trips to Bermuda. "Good morning," smiles her boss, and she replies: "Good morning, Mr. Taylor." She straightens his papers, and she will tell you: "Mr. Taylor is a perfect doll." At the annual jamboree he always asks her to dance, the last dance before he goes home.

But it would be a mistake to judge us by our everyday aspects at the office. Roger Cranford, a dry-as-dust administrator by day, secretly takes piano lessons three times a week before coming to work. He longs to be an artist. Once he served as an overseas political correspondent. He had small by-lines on the radio, but there was an economy wave and . . . Now he walks around our corridors with a pinched expression. He has wedged his driving ambition into a slot far too small to contain it. Frustration impels him to binges of absurd pettiness. He sometimes frustrates and interferes with others, not through malevolence but exasperation. His entire being craves for release from the trivia that surround him. Above all, he hungers for recognition. For that, if everyone were watching him, I think he would have the bravery to ascend to Mars in a balloon. But somehow, because of the inhibition we all share, he could not, if he wanted to, leave the corporate safety island.

Many of us offer small defiances. John Tibbs refuses to
have a telephone in his house. How odd and unreasonable,
no telephone! Yet it is quite easy to understand—John
doesn't want to be reached. He does not care to be available
and checkable. His wife has been distressed at this quirk.
She points out the inconvenience of having to go downstairs
and use the pay phone. John realizes that his foible is a bit
peculiar, but he will not abandon it. The industrial psychologists may nod their heads and make a mark at one end
of their bell graphs, and label John mildly neurotic. Nothing serious though. John—I hear that a few months ago you
sensibly compromised. You now have a phone and permit
only communication *out*. When incoming calls ring at your
house, you do not answer them.

Tall, blonde Alice Carlisle is one of those nervous, efficient
unmarried girls in a man's world. By working harder than
the men in her department she has risen well above the rank
of a secretary. She is pretty in a feverish way. Her eyes shine
with zeal for her job. She studies, she organizes ladies' industrial groups. She does all this with a kind of misplaced
sensual energy that makes you want to say: "Come on,
Alice!" It has generally been assumed that her private life
has been limited by all her industrial activities. But last
year for the first time Alice vacationed in Europe. She spent
three weeks in Spain, and there, she reported on her return,
had a riotous holiday from all that she had ever known. She
twirled with a rose in her teeth and performed challenge
dances with one Spaniard after another. The lessons at the
dance studio in her home town paid off in flamenco routines
that had the audience cheering. The proprietor, she said,
called off the regular floor show and let her go on. She sang
rock 'n roll and gypsy songs, and eventually had to leave hurriedly because the men began fighting over her.

The stories this lonely and excited girl told about her vacation were the kind that evoke a humorous response at the Crystal Palace. One of our girls somehow ought not to have such marvelous experiences. I believe you, Alice. We did what we could in our own minds to cut your Spanish holiday down to size, not out of meanness, but fear—fear that it might be true, for we have declared such uncontrolled revelries out of bounds.

Yet in our time many of us have been rovers and known the edges of life. Ralph Butler, for instance, was an engineer for five years in Turkey and had a mountain girl for a mistress. Arthur Moore led guerrilla troops in the Burmese jungle. On the bridge of a cruiser at Okinawa, Carleton Bell says, "I roared with terror" when a kamikaze leveled out a few inches above his head. Carl Jensen stunted and wire-walked at air shows in the early days. George O'Brien was a cub reporter dancing with excitement at Le Bourget when Lindbergh landed. And in his senior year Robert Cloud actually won the big game with a sixty-yard run.

Today you see such formerly robust individuals, now mild of mien, poking along our corridors in groups and committees with administrative papers in their hands. They have lost something . . . verve . . . appetite. For what? Responsibility. Imagine a decision being walked down the hall by four men, each holding a corner of the authorizing memo. If the matter is of any real significance, in most instances not one of them by himself can earn credit or blame for handling it. Responsibility will be spread all over the place. The question will have been submitted to higher authority and debated there. From the beginning it has been a team effort. The team is responsible for the ultimate good or evil that results from the decision.

From management's point of view this may well be the best

and safest way of doing things. It can also turn bold and free-swinging individuals into little more than administrative couriers. Or as oil magnate J. Paul Getty puts it, glorified office boys. But then nobody is forced to stay in the Crystal Palace. There must be some reason why men of talent as well as mediocrities are content to remain there.

In Maxim Gorki's *The Lower Depths,* miserable people lie about in a dank cellar, and one by one they try to account for the harshness and cruelty of life. Luka the Pilgrim speaks of a man who believed in a land of righteousness. This man, he says, cried out:

"Somewhere on this earth there must be a righteous land—and wonderful people live there . . . good people! They respect each other, help each other, and everything is peaceful and good!"

The man searched vainly for his imaginary land. There was no sign of it on the map, and everybody laughed at him for thinking that there could be such a place. Yet he was only a half-century too early.

Now it may seem almost in bad taste to question the fabulous decency he dreamed about. In our company we have everything this suffering man craved—the respect and help, kind words, everything. How can one be so ungrateful as to complain about decency? But if we feel a genuine need to complain, we can and must.

We are not obliged to celebrate over-comfort simply because its opposite is disastrous. After all, the needs of a man in the Lower Depths may in the long run be no more constant than ours. "To the millions who have to go without two meals a day," said Gandhi, "the only acceptable form in which God dare appear is food." Once he is sure of having enough food, man starts to look around and think of God and happiness in higher terms. Conceivably Gorki's pilgrim, once he reached the righteous land and got back his strength and dignity, might begin to raise his sights.

At the Palace we contend with other poverties. It is no affectation that so many of us feel within ourselves a growing lack of impulse, invention, and desire. The corporation man's vague sense of loss is not trivial. Individuals we remain, but what we sense in common is that we have permitted our wings to be clipped. By trading in our impatience for peace of mind we have sold out not to the devil but to the still, sad music of Muzak. Without knowing it, many of us in the middle ranks suffer, I think, from a loss of pride. Everything has been provided for us. The pilgrim from the Lower Depths wanders in misery. Sequestered in the Middle Depths, we have separated ourselves from a nervous world.

We are in the Middle Depths when we . . .
. . . accept the values and first principles of others without question;
. . . are enchained by property and household appliances;
. . . fall into toils of unnecessary responsibility, and
. . . cannot imagine giving up certain comforts and safeguards.

I would say that the key principle in corporate life is the one governing the annuity and insurance program. This is the frame and prop of all other corporation values. Without it the moral structure of the company, on which life in the Crystal Palace rests, probably could not sustain our operation in its present form.

Who does not believe in the annuity and insurance program? It seems that one would have to be an idiot not to accept this humane and sensible plan. The company matches sixty per cent of your contribution. You can draw out its share as well as yours at any time. The tax collector can't get at the company-contributed portion of your savings for two or three decades. Nothing could be fairer than that.

Virtually all of us at the company do appreciate the benefits system and believe in it. But my friends in the Middle Depths tend to incorporate benefit-thinking and defensive planning into their very psyches, so that the accumulated money becomes the psychological equivalent of an arm or leg, and they fear losing it as they would dread amputation.

The first principle they have accepted here, I think, is that annuities and insurance are *necessary*, whereas they are in fact only *desirable*. And this way of thinking, carried as far as it is carried, may legitimately be questioned. For, once accepted in the mind and heart, the idea that an annuity is as important as (or more important than) your arm or leg will begin to invade the central nervous system. Soon it restricts you in other ways.

The great majority of my friends at company headquarters, for instance, are restricted by property. Heavily mortgaged, they can't move. There follows the familiar installment-buying, which plunges them further into the Middle Depths. One buys a house that is somewhat too expensive, surrounded by rather too much acreage. This means staying put in order to pay for things. The idea seems to be to imprison oneself in responsibility. The Do-It-Yourself enthusiasm is common among our company people. Perhaps it represents an outcropping of individualism. Yet I wonder whether fixing things around the house is not another "responsibility" device to imprison one's free time, apart from achieving absolute security from a ragged lawn or flapping window screen.

As if this were not enough, my friends who are bogged

most securely in the Middle Depths restrict themselves further by producing hordes of children. Or perhaps they just seem to be hordes because they enjoy something approaching equal rights in the family circle. There can be no argument against having children, but I think that corporation people tend for some reason to be too *obliged* to theirs.

Taking care of a family is one thing. But possibly some of us go too far in that direction. We love our families . . . fine. We are, evidently, obliged to provide them with protection undreamed of by our grandfathers. These forms of protection we dare not give up, not under any circumstances. He who inveighs against insurance is a fool. Yet, if necessary, we could do without it. To be dropped out of the company insurance plan would not be the end of the world. Most of us at the Crystal Palace would look on such a prospect with utter horror. Why? Should a more interesting job come up, a job in which we could express ourselves more freely (a job, who knows, that might encourage us to live longer), must we first inquire: "But . . . but what kind of insurance plan do you have?"

Like the Egyptians five hundred years before Christ, we orient toward death; we prepare for old age and garb it in annuities. We dress up death. Our elaborate insurance policies are like the Pharoah's ships absurdly devised to continue dead lives through eternity. But must we not remember also to dress up life in bright costumes? What a *seductio ad absurdam* this defensive planning can become! And it all started back there, that first day, at the indoctrination session when the annuity and insurance man rose to speak.

There is no place among us for a Ulysses. By our standards he was an irresponsible person anyhow. He went voyaging about as if there were no tomorrow. He had no life insurance and sent home no money, and left his wife and family to shift for themselves. Today he would be tracked down and arrested for non-support.

There was a secretary at the Crystal Palace named Roberta Lloyd. She was a tiny wisp, thin and pallid, with an aimlessly good-natured face. Time went by and she was forty years old, coming and going from the suburban apartment where she lived with her parents. You couldn't say much of anything about her, really. She could type on her machine for another twenty years and retire with her savings and pension and thirty-year button, and for all anyone knew another undistinguished life would have run its course.

In the late autumn of one year her friends at the Palace noticed a personality change in this quiescent girl. She took the lead in organizing a company choral group that would sing at the Christmas Party. It was a demanding off-hours enterprise that involved keeping after the volunteer singers to attend rehearsals, obtaining the services of outside professionals to conduct and accompany the group, renting a piano, printing programs, and so on. Roberta pursued the project with a remarkable, almost desperate urgency. At times it seemed to members of the group who gathered for practice sessions in the auditorium that she was working herself into exhaustion, her face was so white and thin. But she sang the carols in a firm clear contralto.

A few weeks before Christmas the company house organ reported: " 'Our rehearsals have been very encouraging,' Miss Lloyd said. "If we progress enough in the next few weeks, we hope to sing for the Orphans' Party, for our own Christmas Party, and possibly do some other engagements.' "

Our Christmas Party is held in a great hotel ballroom. We have cocktails and adjourn to dinner, and then comes the time for dancing. Everybody wants to get out on the floor and have fun. So when the master of ceremonies announced during dessert that the choral group would now give a concert there was a good deal of friendly groaning and raillery as the members proceeded from their various tables to the far end of the hall.

Roberta Lloyd saw that everything was ready. The conductress signaled, the lady at the piano struck a chord, and the singers began "The First Noel." To our surprise they sang beautifully. It was amateur night, but they performed joyfully, with pride in their discipline, in showing us what they could do. There followed "We Three Kings of Orient Are," "God Rest Ye Merry Gentlemen," and "Holy Night." They sang the parts with such feeling that we were caught up in the mood of Christmas. We gave them an ovation and demanded encores, which they gratefully sang.

Applause followed our singers back to their tables. Roberta Lloyd stayed for a few minutes, slipped out to the coat room and went home. Three days later she was in the hospital for an operation, and two weeks after that she was dead.

A photograph of the choral group taken during the Christmas Party performance shows Roberta's indistinct face among the contraltos. Her friends say that she was already feeling some distress in the late autumn. There is nothing in her expression to indicate that she knew death was coming. But she must at least have suspected it.

I feel that in her last days with the company Roberta was trying to escape from the Middle Depths. The imminence of death quickened her life. She made her mark and left a small memory by organizing something beautiful for us while she had time.

III. *It's Cold Out There*

secure I. *vt.* 1. To make secure; protect;
guarantee. 2. To fasten or confine so as
to prevent from getting loose; close. 3. To
get safely in possession; obtain or ac-
quire. . . . II. *a.* 1. Guarded against or
not likely to be exposed to danger. 2. Free
from fear, apprehension, etc.; confident;
careless. 3. Assured; certain; sure. . . .
4. So strong or well made as to render
loss, escape, or failure impossible.
(<L. *securus*, <*se-*, without, + *cura*,
care.)

*Funk & Wagnalls, Desk Standard
Dictionary*

We are bumping along in the company bus on our way from
the railroad station to work. It is quarter-to-nine. We will be
a few minutes late this morning because of the snow. A
three-inch fall last night settled gently on the countryside,
but now powdery gusts are interfering with the driver's
vision.

"It's cold out there!" remarks Lester Jennings. "I pre-
sume the fresh-air fiends will keep the windows shut." This
slow, rosy-faced man has a morbid fear of drafts, or perhaps
it is only a conversation piece with him, every morning, and
also a "characteristic." When you do the same thing every

day within a group of people you develop a characteristic, and everybody identifies you with it. One man puts his nose in the paper, another is habitually cheerful, a third morose; his neighbor discusses politics, and across the aisle this man always disposes of the weather.

"I couldn't have stood it out there much longer!"

The bus kept us waiting for a short time, and we huddled along the sidewalk like a lost battalion, stamping, clutching our ears amid the blowing snow. It is the kind of weather we used to play in for hours when we were children.

The interior of the bus is warm and stuffy. Our breath has condensed on the window panes and you have to polish the glass in order to see outside. But nobody bothers. We nod and read and doze. Some of us are not yet fully awake; others, I think, looking around the bus, will never awaken completely. I see Margaret Hamilton whom I have watched slowly losing her youth in hour-and-a-half commutation rides morning and night for the past three years. Supports her invalid mother, and that is a good thing. But Margaret herself is gradually turning into a good thing. Couldn't she find a job closer to home? Then she might have time for a nap, and wake up prettier and more refreshed—for a date. But then, I forget the savings plan. Once she left the company and withdrew her savings, the protective wall around her would be only half-completed.

Jim Lent stares throughout the ride at stock market quotations. The columns of numbers jump before his eyes. Life appears to reveal itself to this accountant in fields of numbers; he judges things-as-they-are in accordance with the rise and fall and shuffling of numbers. A nice man. I appreciate his cheerful good-morning before he disappears into that page. But I have seen him in the spring when the bus windows are open; there are glistening ripples in the black brooks along the roadside; the dogwood is beginning to flower, and he never looks up from the financial section.

Actually, it occurs to me, it is true of all of us in the bus, morning and evening: we are seldom aware of the here and now while we are riding in this company carriage. We know exactly where we have been and where we are going; we could set our watches by the arrival of stoplights and the familiar stretches of landscape that pass by. The gentle bumping of our transportation induces drowsiness. Our thoughts wander or drift into indistinct patterns. Thus you ride for years over the same road in the back seat of someone else's vehicle.

Our driver accelerates his bus through bitter cold and shifting curls of snow. Without a doubt we will be delivered in ten minutes to the Palace's steam-heated front steps. Looking around at all the passive faces, I think what a peaceful load of humanity we are, so innocent, so sure of the years ahead. If one of us, willing to be a disturber of the peace, would rise from his seat and cry out: "Wake up! Prisoners of Benevolence!"

And yet . . . how many thousands of managers and workers on the outside would happily change places with us, and never mind mediocrity and dullness—simply to arrive at our peace of mind. Admit that the corporate structure, with its quiet, orderly procedures, has not come into being by chance. Our kind of company exists in its present form partly in response to our own demand. We asked for Social Justice. An enlightened corporation has provided it for us in the best way management knows how—by creating a private welfare state.

It was not foreseen that we might wither for lack of challenge. But perhaps some of us were sick of challenge, sick of competition. A constant testing of adequacy keeps you alive, but it frays the nerves too. If you have no stomach for this sort of thing, seek protection within our gates. The Crystal Palace is a rampart against the brutalities of free enterprise.

I think back on earlier days in the city. In the beginning I had the instincts of a clerk, and did my best in a nervous way to satisfy my superiors. At that time, I imagined free enterprise in terms of the familiar parable, according to Matthew. A master gave each of his servants a certain number of talents, and they profited in varying amounts, except for one poor-spirited man who buried his paltry talent and didn't use it. The master, in denouncing him, said:

"Take therefore the talent from him, and give it unto him which hath ten talents. For unto every one that hath shall be given, and he shall have abundance: but from him that hath not shall be taken away even that which he hath. And cast ye the unprofitable servant into outer darkness . . ."

I was an unprofitable servant with a buried talent, and how I feared the outer darkness! I had a recurring dream that I would end up some day on the top floor of a men's rooming house sitting on my bed in an old undershirt listening to the radio—and occasionally looking out the window to watch young people drive by in open convertibles. I would be a clerk in a mail order house, the equivalent of a goose quill pusher, like Bob Cratchit, with a tyrannical young supervisor ordering me about. This could still happen, but not so long as I stay at the Palace. Such dreams no longer visit me since I have been there.

A mighty fortress is our Palace; I will not want for anything. I may live my days without humiliation. I will not be fired. It nourishes my self-respect. I am led along the paths of righteousness for my own good. I am protected from tyrants. It guards me against tension and fragmentation of my self. It anoints me with benefits. Though we pass through hard times, I will be preserved. These strong walls will surely embrace all the days of my life, if I remain a corporation man forever.

The wind howls outside. The driver points to an accident on the road, and we polish our window panes. Our bus rolls by a car that has skidded into a ditch. Its owner fortunately is equipped with ear muffs. He swings his arms and walks up and down. His mournful face is twisted against the cold, as he watches the crew of a salvage truck attach a line to his back bumper.

"It's rough out there!" repeats Lester Jennings happily, with a small variation of his theme.

So it can be. Perhaps we ought to stop complaining and count our blessings.

The Palace protects me from unemployment. Do you remember how it feels to be out of a job in difficult circumstances? I do, and I will never be able to put certain humiliations out of my memory. My money slowly ran out until the last nickel disappeared.

Then comes the time for pawning things, and of course they are never worth a tenth of what you suppose. The pawnbrokers and secondhand booksellers know you, and drive the price down to a pathetic level because you have no bargaining power and become as defenseless as a rabbit. I sold all my books, walking around the town to different stores so that, if possible, the same dealer would not be able to look down his nose at me twice.

"I've been broke, but I've never been poor," said Mike Todd. He had boldness and brass under fire. But not all of us have the power to summon up a devil-may-care manliness in bad times. We should have, but we don't. The next thing one pawns is self-respect.

You call up one of your friends and make a date to see him. Immediately this is a lie. You don't want to see him. You want his money. Finally, shamefacedly you slip in your request for a loan. The expression on his face changes; it always does. He knows that you have been forced into the position of being a fraud and he is embarrassed for you. Usually you get the money. In fact, he is sorry that it can't be more. Obligations press him too. Say he has always been a good friend, but your relationship with him may never be quite the same again.

The process is repeated, and the word gets around. Everybody is courteous, in the beginning anyhow, although their tones of voice become somewhat guarded when they talk to you. At one point I thought: "Pull yourself together. You're not the only man who has ever been out of a job. Back off from it, get your perspective, make jokes . . . be attractive."

A good suggestion and hard to follow. You can't easily back off and look at your condition philosophically, because the sin of poverty is with you every hour of the day. How to back off from what surrounds you, confronts and crowds you, settles in the very clothes you wear, thins your body and hollows your eyes?

Further, after a while you begin to sense that your plight has become aesthetically displeasing to others. In the phrase, one "cuts a sorry figure." It is an assignment for Hercules to be attractive when people are afraid that you will try to borrow money.

Freud recalls:

"The story about the baron who, having been deeply

touched by the shnorrer's (beggar's) tale of woe, rang
for his servants and said: 'Throw him out of the house;
he is breaking my heart.' " [1]

I found that, unconsciously or not, the people I met were
touched by my ill fortune but also resented, as it were, the
rags of failure. The jobless one becomes a walking reproach
to those who have an extra twenty-five dollars in their pock·
ets. Having a natural desire not to part with money, at least
not more than once, his friends give him the next best
thing—advice. What a dreadful visitation that is! George M.
Cohan said: "Never give advice unless you can give money
with it." (Another phrasing of the same thought: "Put your
money where your mouth is.") Right. I won't easily forget
the sumptuous helpings of advice that were heaped on me;
the questions like: "Why are you so thin?"; or, helpfully:
"You're not looking well, you know."

Who should look well? In this ego-crunching situation—
which I need never, never go through again—a man has all
he can do to get up in the morning. Life becomes a constant
struggle for dignity. It is not so much that others go out of
their way to diminish your ego. You do it yourself, and they
only respond to your own marked-down self-esteem.

Without realizing it, I began volunteering to run errands,
call the taxi, buy the beer, bring up a newspaper. What
could be more natural after a while than for people, again
without thinking, to turn to the over-accommodating jobless
man when these things had to be done?

Now, some years later, I have had the experience of being
on the fortunate side of the line. I have felt prosperous and
slipped a man twenty dollars, and seen the way he looks at
me—with mingled gratitude and resentment.

1 From *Wit and Its Relation to the Unconscious.*

Resentment is a natural reaction when one's very manhood has been called into question. "Weighed and found wanting" is the expression. Since free enterprise of any kind is a stern test of manhood, when I fail, even temporarily, I become an embarrassment upon the earth. The ego at such times is a castle under siege. Circumstances one by one are breaking down the iron doors, infiltrating into the kitchen . . . and sometimes into the bedroom. A man's ability to make love can be sadly reduced, and even blocked out altogether for a while, if his pride has been bashed around enough.

In the midst of all this you are filling out employment forms and being interviewed for jobs. Eventually you land one, as I did. But the preceding weeks were rough. I was staying with a married couple. Although we were close friends, my continuing presence in their little apartment was too much. They had practically no money. I lacked not only a penny but a decent pair of pants, and had to borrow my friend's pants in order to go job-hunting. There came a day when he couldn't lend me those. All I had then was a torn pair of army issue, and I thought, looking at the holes in them: "This is inadequacy."

We were not joyous like bohemians in our poverty and incompetence, but sullen and despairing most of the time, even though flashes of comradeship occasionally relieved the tension. My friend, a good and kind young man by nature, was unhappily caught in the middle, for his wife could not bear to have me there. She also was a naturally fine person, but infuriated by our general atmosphere of failure. While I stayed away from the apartment as much as I could, there was always the possibility of the bedraggled guest blundering in at the wrong time.

I mention these things to show the risks of free enterprise in terms of personal dignity. Multiply these relatively mild misfortunes a thousand times and spread them among many thousands of people and we can sense one reason why the corporation, with its orderliness and concern for human dignity, has a most attractive side.

I sit in our bus with my comfortable business companions and the respectable girls with dull eyes, and try to understand why I sometimes look back sentimentally on those nervous days. Perhaps I miss luck . . . chance. The protected man doesn't need luck; therefore, it seldom visits him. He misses the excitement of having his life turn on a surprise stroke of fortune, good or bad. There were also certain illuminations that never come now.

During that bad period I had one ace in the hole which I didn't want to turn up unless it was absolutely necessary. It was a postage stamp, canceled at the site of the first (1946) atomic bomb test at Bikini. Since there were only a few thousand of them, they would be of significant value as the years went by. I had planned to save it for twenty years, but now there was no time. My friend's wife was out. I told him about the stamp and we went off to sell it, planning a big celebration that night. Wouldn't she be surprised!

As we walked across town a terrific thunderstorm gathered, and a deluge fell on us. I hurriedly put the envelope back into my wallet, and we ran through the downpour in our threadbare clothes, so wet immediately that it didn't make any difference.

"Careful! Don't let it get wet."

"No, it's all right."

"Don't wrinkle it!"

"No, no."

We burst into the stamp exchange. It was a luxurious place with thick red carpets and rows of display cases, as dignified as a bank or museum. The distinguished philatelists looked over the two specimens dripping on the carpet, and after a moment one of them approached.

"I have a stamp. It's quite rare."

"Yes?"

I produced it, saying: "The letter makes it valuable. See the postmark."

He turned it over in his hand, and we waited.

"How much do you estimate . . . ?"

"If it were in good condition," said the man, "I would give you fifteen cents." He returned the envelope to me and walked away.

We went outside where the downpour had increased to a cascade of rain. Thunder and lightning were cracking all over the city. We looked at each other and said exactly the same thing: "The hell with it," and walked very slowly down the middle of the street letting the rain drench us completely. With that, the entire afternoon and the storm became an enormous luxury, it seemed, that only we could enjoy. Everyone ran into stores and apartment houses, and rushed to any shelter. Drivers blinded by the rain pulled to the curb. Practically everything stopped. There were the traffic policemen, like shining black towers in their raincoats, and ourselves. Having nothing, we were free to be idiotic. The storm went on for fifteen minutes; the rain at one point seemed not to fall but to be solid. We strolled in this. Our clothes were a mass of wet wash. The water in the streets ran over our ankles. But we were the only ones not huddled under cover. We felt without speaking of it a marvelous identity, a sense of I, I am here. Even after arriving home we experienced the feeling for quite a while, of being in some way important.

Now the company bus pauses at our last intersection.

Through the snowy branches of the woodlands I see the Crystal Palace on the hilltop. It appears nearly to touch the bright cumulus clouds. A car alongside honks and I wave to Dick Smithson and the gang in his car pool. He waves back and makes a gesture of helplessness, pointing to his watch. We are going to be late. Of course, he is pretending concern. Few of us have ever so much as been reprimanded.

I am preserved from tension and fragmentation. One of the privileges of free enterprise, as opposed to the private welfare state, is that of working for or under a business maniac.

The maniac is an energetic, highly intelligent businessman, lacking in humanity, who immerses himself completely in his job, has virtually no life outside his job, and expects you not to have either. Such men flourish because they are oriented toward their work all the time. Anything besides work has no meaning for them. Frequently pleasing and even charming, they do not really believe that other people exist. Others are the population of their dreams. Since dreams must be managed and coaxed, they *talk* to you and say all the words as though you existed. They may want to breathe life into you, but only in the sense that a playwright struggles to bring his characters alive as he orders them about.

These sick men, piling small enterprises on top of large ones, have helped make us into a great country. If the accumulation of details makes for greatness, maniacs are in their element. They will devote their monstrous energies to the most trivial matters that would bore anyone else to death. Consequently they often become terrible bosses. Savagely pursuing details into the late hours of the night, driving or persuading their inferiors to keep up with them, they are genuinely bewildered by the softness of the man who wants to go home and the softness of women who ask when *they* are coming home.

A predatory sport in a pinstriped suit may build his empire in a button factory, an advertising agency, or a used car lot . . . but he will not make my life miserable at the Crystal Palace. He will not be there. There is no one at the Palace to rack my nerves, give me indigestion, make me so sick and tired that I can't love my family, try to force me into believing in something trivial, and failing that, fire me—no one.

Across the aisle, poor, fortunate Lester Jennings declares to nobody in particular: "We're gettin' there!" A talentless man, he cranes his neck as if to catch a glimpse of his pension down the road. Security has aged him; at fifty he is out of the race. Lester has one strength left, insofar as being a person is concerned. Our corporation has given him the priceless treasure of dignity.

I am thinking of frightened older men with no Crystal Palace to protect them. I remember, more than ten years ago, Mr. Walter Mason.

It was a time of competence for me. Somewhat toughened and ambitious, I was a junior copywriter with the Barnes & Ainsworth advertising agency. I worked hard, and accepted all the values of advertising. We had a two-man creative staff. When our chief copywriter resigned to start his own business I hoped to take his place. Although I had but two years' experience, it wasn't impossible. The account executives liked me, as did many of our clients. The dream of promotion ended a week later with a mimeographed notice on the bulletin board.

"We are pleased to announce the appointment of WALTER MASON as copy chief. Our agency is fortunate in gaining the services of a man of Mr. Mason's stature.

...responsible for the brand name of Oh Boy cereals. Mr. Mason will be in direct charge of all the creative activities performed by this agency. Account executives will look to him for leads and suggestions, and will consult closely with him in planning and developing campaigns in all media."

Ambition thwarted, I immediately worked up a resentment against the pretentious fellow who was to be my new boss. I imagined him urbane and witty, putting me in my place with a few casual words. It turned out exactly that way.

The agency president, Mr. Ray Barnes, called me into his office. He was an elegant gentleman from Baltimore who looked like an itinerant gambler. Despite his courtly manner, there was something cheap about him. His smile and narrow eyes were perfectly merciless. Seeing him, I would think of Mack the Knife and the line now translated: "Oh, the shark has pretty teeth, dear . . ." I liked him though, because he was smart.

Beside him sat a nervous old person.

"Walt," said Mr. Barnes, "here's the young fellow."

Walter Mason adjusted his rimless spectacles: "Well, I see that I shall have to look up to him, at least in a physical sense."

I measured a small scarecrow of a man with wispy hair and faded blue eyes, who had been ill. Even now an in-

...ver since Jack left ...he hasn't panicked. Of course, ...find that he's got a lot to learn—"

"I trust that we will be able to remedy that," said Mr. Mason.

"I think so," I said, looking at him directly.

We were already enemies. It was the only relationship we could possibly have because I knew his secret, and my manner clearly told him so. Apparently no one else had an inkling of it, but I recognized at once that my new copy chief had lost his confidence, and was a has-been, and that he was finished. Therefore, from the wolfish viewpoint of the young, he was a fake. I saw him purely as he was at the moment, without giving him credit for what he had been. The others, because they were sophisticated, could be taken in by Walter Mason's press clippings. But since I hadn't the least understanding of how hard it is to *stay* successful, I made no allowances. What difference did it make what he had done in the past? To hell with Dover cigarettes. I had no charity for him. All I could see before me was a trembling, unconfident oldster hiding behind a front of sarcasm; someone who didn't have it anymore . . . in my way.

This knowledge gave me a sure and peaceful feeling. I was merely surprised that such a tired old man, using the false credentials of the past, had managed to deceive the agency into accepting his eminence.

My face must have had a sullen cast. Ray Barnes regarded me sternly and said: "Look to Mr. Mason for guidance. He's forgotten more about copy than most of us will ever know."

Walter Mason coughed and fussed among his papers. "Well," he said, "I hope not."

Within a few days our relationship had worsened. Crabbed age and youth cannot live together, especially in an advertising agency. I was impatient with his air of superiority. He had a status that he was desperately trying to defend. Our aversion for one another had to extend to all things. He saw my dull shoes and told me to get a shine. I saw his face as a symbol of incompetent and sick authority under the fluorine lamps. He saw a towering young man following him about with a frigid expression. I saw a rattletrap old fraud gallivanting around the office and trying to make friends by means of schoolteacherish wisecracks, now and then at my expense.

"You know, Smitty . . ." he winked at an account executive who had come upon us while we were disagreeing over a piece of copy. "You know what they say?"

"What do they say, Walt?"

"You can always tell a Boston man," said Mr. Mason, "but you can't tell him much."

"Yes you can!" I protested. "But I just don't get this approach. I wish you'd *show* me what you mean."

This was a not very subtle attempt to put him in the position of having to write some copy on his own. So far he had confined himself to blue-penciling mine.

He liked to hold a ruler and lay it on his palm each time he made a point. "It's very simple; just sit right down to it. The essence of good copywriting is speed. Don't think too much —let the thoughts flow through you."

"I can't go along with that completely," I said.

"You will some day," he smiled. "Now be off with you. Smitty and I must put our heads together."

That old impostor! He became an obsession with me, and

I with him. Every day was a battle between youth and age. He rode me.

"Well, well, in your studies of literature, have some authors perhaps inspired you?"

I mentioned Thomas Wolfe.

"Oh, that one. He had no terminal facilities."

"Have you ever written anything, Mr. Mason? I mean, creatively."

"I," he said, "wrote a detective story to end all detective stories."

"Apparently it didn't." (But this was said in my imagination.)

Several times a day my phone would ring and the dry voice would summon me four steps across the hall.

"It's not a bad memorandum you have there. Rather on the impetuous side, but interesting. Here's one passage I don't understand. You say: 'The rest of the program may be presented verbally.' "

"Yes?"

"Don't you mean *orally?*"

"Either way you like," I said.

"But it's not either way. It must be the right way. I'm sure you agree to that."

Eventually we looked it up in the dictionary, and there was a small difference, and I was wrong. It was exasperating to be caught out on this detail—a paltry bit of knowledge he had used like a bar trick.

All of this time he had managed to avoid writing copy. Instead he meticulously edited mine, which until he came along had seldom been changed very much. A certain amount of editing is the rule in an agency, no matter how effective the copy may be. But there comes a point when the copywriter is edited, in a lint-picking way, to such an extent that he loses confidence. He begins to hesitate before putting any word down.

Walter Mason had made his reputation as a copywriter during a period when they did not write complete sentences. The time of the fashionable incomplete sentence had long since passed, but he didn't know it. He was forever putting dots in my copy and crossing out personal pronouns. Thus, something like:

> "Have You Discovered Caribbean—
> The Rum With A *Punch?*"

would become:

> "Man Alive! . . . Discovered Caribbean? . . .
> Heard Others Talk About It? . . . Care
> To Try A Glass? . . . It's The Rum With A
> PUNCH. . . ."

"Dots are dramatic," he said. "They catch the eye, and that's what counts."

The constant mutilation of my sentences made me furious.

"What's the matter, boy?" our art director asked me one day.

"I've got dots before my eyes," I said bitterly, showing him Mr. Mason's handiwork.

"Well, I wouldn't worry. Don't worry, boy," he said.

"What do you mean, don't worry?"

He grinned and walked down the corridor singing: "There'll be some changes made."

I hoped so. "Sooner or later the old fraud will have to write something," I consoled myself. It was noticeable too that some of our account men smiled the wrong way at his sallies. God strafe him with failure. I waited for Walter Mason to fall on his face.

It was spring and the scent of a new campaign was in the air. To my joy, the word came down that the presentation to our cigarette-lighter account was so important that Walter Mason himself would have to draw it up. His task would be to work out the general approach and then write the copy for three pilot advertisements.

All that week his door was closed as he worked toward the Friday deadline. I hardly saw him, but I heard him. His typewriter would rattle furiously; there would be a long interval of silence, and then the sound of paper being torn out of the machine.

Friday morning came and still he was not done. I heard him on the phone trying to put it off until Monday morning, but from his tone I could gather that they weren't having any of that.

"All right, Ray!" I heard his voice. "All right, six! Fine!"

The afternoon went by. Now he had two hours to go. The tempo of his machine became frantic. He was gunning fragments of thought in short bursts. There was an angry x-ing out of the last sentence, then nothing . . . and the savagery of crumpled paper. Across the corridor I could actually hear him breathing, and then something like a groan.

I thought: "The poor bastard." Perhaps I could help him. But then I remembered his schoolmasterly airs, and said to myself: "No, let the bastard come to me."

I lit a cigarette and looked out the window. At five o'clock the girls hurried through the corridors. The time clock was bonging as, one by one, they punched out. The men followed more slowly. There were a few isolated bongs, and the office grew quiet. The late afternoon sun blazed on our frosted glass cubicles, then abruptly disappeared behind a building, and our floor was in shadow. Ray Barnes came by and gave me his fixed smile. He went on down to his office. I thought: "When the shark bites with his teeth, dear . . ." I heard him greet the two executives in charge of the cigarette-lighter account. Stepping into the hallway, I saw them at the long conference table. Ray Barnes had just looked at his watch. My enemy's presentation was due in forty-five minutes. I waited.

There was no sound from Walter Mason's office. I was wondering: "What's he doing in there?" when his door opened and I was confronted by the face of a desperate old man gazing across the corridor at me. His appearance startled me. I had never seen anyone look like that. He seemed to have no defense at all. His collar was open; his shirt was damp and dirty and falling out over his belt. His arms hung at his sides. In one hand he clutched a disorderly sheaf of papers. Surely he wasn't going to submit that mess.

I didn't get up from my chair. We exchanged a glance that recognized everything. He came into my office and said: "Well, well, still here, I see. Strange that you should be here tonight."

"Oh, I'm just hanging around, cleaning up a few things."

"I see. Well, since you're available, might as well put you to work. Here!" He flung his papers on my desk. "Let's have the youth angle," he said sarcastically. Crumpled in the visitor's chair, he looked as if he weighed sixty pounds. He closed his eyes while I read.

It was rotten and it was hopeless. Whatever creative juices this poor man had ever possessed were dried up. Or perhaps fear had dried him up. The sentences were hollow with spurious good cheer, but worse, they were inept. All copywriters know the times when words become one's enemies rather than allies. Mason's words were stumbling buffoons when he tried to be lighthearted and clods dragging heavy weights when he attempted seriousness. Throughout I came upon a curious, fumbling lack of elementary skill. Even his grammar was awkward. The paragraphs took bad bounces, and sibilants here and there had been strung together in a way that made the copy almost impossible to read aloud. Amid all this the frantic writer had taken fistfuls of dots . . . and flung them into the stew apparently at random.

I turned over the last page. He opened his eyes and regarded me with such despair that my rancor vanished and I felt nothing but pity for him.

"Well, Mr. Mason . . ."

"Ah," he said, "it's a bit rough in spots—you don't have to tell me."

I didn't have to tell him. What was the use? Given time I could have salvaged a bit of it. With less than a half-hour before the presentation nothing could be done.

"Do you have any thoughts?" he asked.

"The message is clear enough. The tone . . . I think I would change—"

"The tone, yes. What do you suggest?"

I don't know why I said: "You know more about these things than I do, Mr. Mason."

"Ah hah!" He glanced at me with a flash of amusement in his eyes, then gathered up his papers and went back across the corridor. I watched him putting on his jacket and knotting his tie. Then he was plodding through the dark recesses of the office toward the lighted conference room.

On Monday I was dispatched to the factory of one of our clients to take notes on the manufacture of a new product. I didn't return to the agency until nearly closing time, and went immediately to the account executive's office to report on what I had seen. We talked for a short while. When I came out the office was darkened, but there was a light in Walter Mason's room behind his closed door. I knocked eagerly, wanting, of course, to find out how the presentation had gone.

He was sitting with his hands in his lap, bowed forward, and I had the impression of a small, old face and little shoulders. His desk was bare except for a pink slip on the green blotter.

He looked up and said: "I have been summarily dismissed."

"You mean—just now?" I was as stupefied as he was.

"It's incredible. No one spoke to me. I went away for a few minutes, and came back to find *this* . . ." He indicated the slip of paper on his blotter.

The cowardly dismissal chilled me. They hadn't dared, or thought it worth bothering, to administer it face-to-face. I had not imagined that the Pink Slip actually existed.

"Not a bone of satisfaction," he said. "Not so much as a bone."

"Oh, Mr. Mason!" I said, like a schoolboy.

With that he pulled himself together. "Well, well, don't look so downhearted. It's part of the game, as you no doubt will discover some day."

He went to the coat rack and flung over his shoulders a curious garment that I had never seen anyone wear outside the movies. It was a light black cloak. He fastened it at the neck and turned quickly so that the folds whirled around his shrunken body, and he resembled a feeble old inadequate nobleman.

In the elevator we didn't speak. On the sidewalk he hailed a cab. He waved me in, saying: "I will take you to your lodgings." As he huddled, crumpled in his cloak in the back seat of the cab, remorse attacked me. I thought: "I could have helped him. I've done my best to ruin an old man."

Our relationship was fated to end unhappily, for on climbing out of the taxi I made the terrible mistake of saying: "Let me pay for this . . ." He gave me a furious look and slammed the door.

"North!" he commanded the driver, and the cab rolled away.

As the company bus pulls up before the front steps of the Crystal Palace, I think how Walter Mason would have gone down on his knees and begged, if his pride had let him, for the chance to enjoy his declining business years with us. I can see him—puttering around, favoring us with his old saws and high-buttoned-shoes humor. A somewhat tedious veteran he would be, but with his honor intact and no pity necessary, and the green fields and fishing rod a year or two away. As it was, he died a few years after leaving the agency.

It is easy to talk of suffering as though it were some divine flagellation for one's own good. Adversity is indeed educational . . . but for old men it offers no payoff.

Lester Jennings remarks, always to no one in particular: "Well, I guess we made it." We pile out of the bus and run up the front steps of the Crystal Palace through rising clouds of steam. Despite the weather, it isn't cold at all.

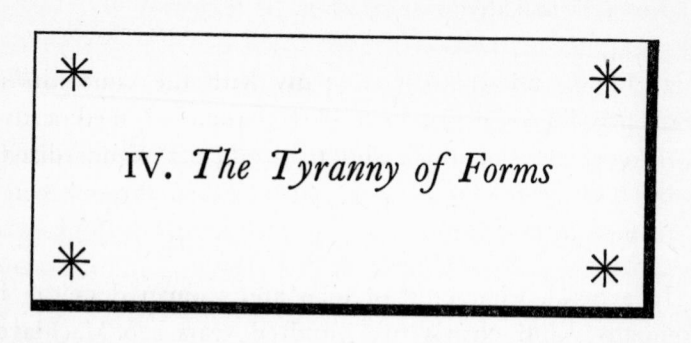

IV. *The Tyranny of Forms*

A bank, said Bob Hope, is a place that will lend you money if you can prove that you don't need it. Similarly, a corporation prefers to offer a job to a man who already has one, or doesn't immediately need one. The company accepts you if you are already accepted. To obtain entry into paradise, in terms of employment, you should be in a state of grace.

To make sure that you *are* a graceful person, and to screen out potential malefactors, the company's personnel and placement specialists use all kinds of pretesting devices. These vary in detail from one corporation to another, but they are likely to involve a series of interviews; your résumé; a searching employment form in which you account for yourself from high school and college years to the present; psychological tests, and at many companies, cunningly contrived spotchecks of your behavior under stress.

Some of these obstacle courses offer reasonable challenges. Others, as we shall see, actually treat the job applicant as though he were a mental patient. All corporate hiring practices, it seems to me, whether they are reasonable or not, have two characteristics in common:

1. They represent an extraordinary downgrading of the intuitive faculty that keeps the relationship between man and man alive and exciting.

2. They tend to fill a company with the same kinds of people; to maintain a slow parade of mediocrity through the corridors, and to produce a standardized intelligence that must eventually weaken through continuous inbreeding.

In general, what kind of man and woman does the big company want? Nearly five hundred years ago Machiavelli advised "The Prince" on the proper selection of his administrators:

> "There are three different kinds of brains, the one understands things unassisted, the other understands things when shown by others, the third understands neither alone nor with the explanation of others. The first kind is most excellent, the second also excellent, but the third useless."

Interestingly enough, for the purposes of maintaining an organization, Machiavelli rates the second kind of intelligence—the one that understands things when shown by others—virtually on a par with that of the man who can think for himself. I believe most corporation personnel departments would go along with this evaluation, although, of course, they would never admit it. In fact, the employee who is content to "understand things when shown by others" seems to be the kind they generally do hire. Such a person, we know, may be of more immediate value to the organization than someone who insists on his intellectual rights.

Only in a limited sense do corporations like the Crystal

Palace formulate their own hiring policies. Instead they follow (and modify to their own needs) policies developed by industrial psychologists. These specialists in turn shape *their* systems to meet the corporations' requirements. A scientific whirligig takes place here as the corporations and the psychologists solemnly chase each other's premises.

I think of personnel specialists as tailors. Instead of fitting a suit to a man, they tailor a man into a slot. No alterations are permitted. If his talents bulge out of the slot here and there, or if it seems that he may rattle about in it, out he goes. The personnel men stand around smiling, polite and considerate, holding their tape measures, while we try on the job. They are indeed likely to be sympathetic, because the job specifications are not theirs. The form into which we must fit has been determined by someone at the Mt. McKinley Business School.

This is the sad thing—seldom in job interviews can we be ourselves, and have a straight relationship with one another, because all the forms and tests and specifications get in the way. Occasionally a personnel officer, through his own warm qualities, can break through the "human engineering" paraphernalia that surround the interview. At the Crystal Palace we have such a man. He really tries to know you; he has a generous intelligence. But even he must take into account the standardized thinking of the people upstairs. He can't afford to recommend too many unusual characters.

When I came to the Palace, needing the job badly, I had good luck. I filled out the forms, of course, but avoided the psychological tests. (I had a strong introduction. Also, although our company has tests available, it does not worship them blindly as some corporations do.) My only trouble came from a young assistant in the personnel section. He went over my record of previous employment with a cold eye. I thought I had hidden the gaps pretty well, but he found them.

"What's this? What's this?"

"Yes?"

"Here in 1948—there's no firm coverage at all."

"Oh, then," I said. That was when I had sold my books, had no pants, and had once bought for twenty-nine cents a can of something called all-purpose food which guaranteed to keep you alive for a week. "Then," I said, "I decided to look around. I wasn't too happy with what I was doing."

"But that went on for . . . nine months!"

"About that, I guess."

He looked at me for a number of seconds, and then said in a softly inquiring tone: "It must have been hard for you."

Without thinking—the best way—I answered indifferently: "Oh no, I had plenty of money."

It worked. Wanting the truth, he got back the lie he forced me to tell him, and he accepted it. But, watchful young man, can you imagine how I felt about you at that moment? Why couldn't you deal with the flesh-and-blood person before you . . . not the hole in that silly employment record? Suppose I had not been given the grace to reply: "I had plenty of money" in an unconcerned tone? If I had started telling you about all-purpose food. . . .

All of us who hold jobs at the Crystal Palace are screened people. We are the pretested, predigested people. Many were called, but we were chosen. How? And what is the thinking beind this selective process?

The downgrading of intuition. Once, long ago it seems, hiring was done in a rough and ready way. It still is, by firms that are too small to maintain an employee-relations staff. Or by companies that expect a certain amount of turnover.

When I and my friends started looking for jobs in 1940, most of us were accepted or turned away on the basis of a personal interview and our record of experience. That was all. The interview was of the greatest importance. *I* talked to *you*. We sized each other up. We did what is now called a take on one another. Eventually the decision was in effect: "Sorry, but you won't do," or "Young man, I like your style. We'll give you a tryout."

Employer and applicant made an intuitive connection. By intuition I mean perception through unconscious logic. We tried to see into each other, beyond the things we said, behind the polite formalities. We sought to discover what the other was really like. Sometimes one was the victim of whimsical judgments. A businessman I know always scrutinized a visitor's shoes in order to determine his character. He could, he said, "read" an applicant by studying his footwear, the shine, the repair of the heels, and so on. Another, after World War II, despised anyone who had been in the Air Force. He was a former infantryman and had once been bombed and wounded by our own planes.

Naturally the hit-or-miss hiring system had uneven results. Frequently the new employee couldn't do the job, or a good man was hired for the wrong job. If he failed, he was let go. It was as simple as that. This unscientific procedure at its worst wrought a good deal of misery. Bang! One was out of a job. It created clash and anger, and that great American line: "You can't fire me! I quit!" (Who hears that anymore; it has gone, along with Fourth of July firecrackers.)

But these intuitive hiring methods also produced a dashing, vigorous, and personal conduct of business. Above all, it was personal. There was no system interposed between us. If I rubbed you the wrong way, we rubbed. If we became friends, we earned our friendship. We were not pretested associates fitted together by employment counselors like so many blocks.

In an intuitive situation, *you* do the work. In a scientific milieu, you feed data into machines and formulas, and *they* do the work. This is all very well for computing the trajectories of missiles—but a man is not yet a guided missile.

The mania for pretesting. The hiring practices we have now reflect a trend in American life that has been developing through the 1950's. This tendency involves a growing distrust of imagination. We see evidence of it everywhere, for example, in medicine. I have heard medical men bemoan the decline of diagnostic ability among our doctors. They are said to rely too heavily on machines and tests, to lean on machines. Now it may be that this is an old wives' tale spread by disgruntled patients who have to pay for all these tests. Also, if my life were in jeopardy, I would certainly welcome a blood analysis or two to confirm the physician's diagnosis, if he has made one . . . and if I didn't bleed to death meanwhile. The point here is not to question the doctors' methods but to note that diagnosis from imagination has yielded to some extent (as perhaps it well should, except in an emergency) to diagnosis after tests.

Distrust of imagination has been fashionable for some years in advertising and public relations. The familiar Motivational Research has done away with the intuitions and visions of the copywriter in many agencies. Why have a man do the work when a survey, or a fast depth analysis, seems to hit the target with hardly a margin for error? Oscar Wilde's perception that life imitates art must be amended. Today life is imitating science.

At the Crystal Palace you may see the predigestion of mankind going on week after week—in the form of multiple interviews and multiple testings of job candidates. No one, it seems, dares to be wrong anymore. Or perhaps the idea now is that no single person can be right about anything; that the decision must be made by a group in order to be valid. At any rate, when the poor cob comes up our front steps everybody must get into the act of evaluating his resources. (This also helps spread responsibility if a mistake *is* made.)

Tom, Dick, and Harry interview him in turn, and scribble their own chicken tracks on his various forms. Each of the sorcerer's apprentices naturally feels that he must earn his salary by adding his own modest but shrewd appraisal of the soul before him. So the applicant is viewed through a half-dozen lenses. As he is being chatted with, the dimensions of his personality are matched against the cardboard cutout, or the slot, which is the job. A multiple judgment, a dossier made up of opinions, forms, and tests piles up around him. The net result: he is observed and tabulated to such an extent that this *man*, the one with his hat in his hand, you, me, John McGee, is really seen by NOBODY. His capacities and aptitudes are seen, but *he* isn't.

How can you come to know a man by means of the "Standardized Interview" or "Non-Directive Questioning?" The first pours your talk into a predetermined formal order; the second is designed through careful phrasing to *bring out* the job-seeker, to make him talk. Well, he will follow your order and he will talk, no doubt, as you want him to. But curiously enough, with all these psychological maneuverings directed toward the discovery of a human being, an element of humanity is missing. You, the interviewer, are the missing element—for the interviewer naïvely expects to receive honest personal answers to contrived impersonal questions.

"It must have been hard for you." This was a non-directive comment. The phrase is not exactly a question, yet it demands an explanation. The interviewer pretends to be concerned. Through this pretense, which he has learned in school, he hopes to get at the truth. But the sham is transparent. The candidate well knows that his questioner is faking concern. Therefore, confronted with this standardized interest in his past, he lies. He rearranges his experience to suit the interviewer. We have a strange situation here.

We have a method interviewing a man. We have an ultimate nondirection. For "non-directive" is also non-involved, nonengaged because it is non-natural, nonhuman. Will the *interviewer* be equipped to understand a human response when he is serving in the capacity of an instrument—when he puts questions that have been shaped by a scientist in another part of the country? I am sure that the standardized interview has all kinds of validity behind it, but who on earth really (as opposed to faking a conversation) talks to others in this way? Did you ever make a friend or an enemy—or even an acquaintance—by non-directive questioning? This is a technique that may fairly be used, say, by psychiatrists on emotionally disturbed patients. They are not trying to "know" the patient; they want to know his symptoms. These are two very different matters.

Knowing a person is a two-way process. You have to kick things around a bit, with both of you giving, both of you open, both being yourselves. Pattern interviewing is purely extractive. It is scientific. Now this may be fine for the psychologist, for he has no intention of associating with the patient, either as a friend or business acquaintance. He will not have to live with him or work with him.

Once a man is hired, the corporation *will* associate with him, presumably for the next twenty-five to forty years. This indeed is the major reason why hiring practices have become so formalized—science is called in to guard against a dreadful long-term mistake being made. But observe the twofold irrelevancy of judging an applicant by standardized interviews, non-directive techniques, forms and tests.

You have an interviewer pretending to be a person, and an applicant pretending to be what he is not. They are both talking past each other to the Mt. McKinley Business School. The average applicant, after all, is not so stupid. He can usually sense whether he is talking across the desk to a man, or to a servant of somebody else's method. Therefore, to land the job, he does his best to turn himself into the image that the job wants.

Behold! An inanimate thing, the job, has desire. An inanimate thing, the form, makes demands. Animate beings, the interviewer and job-hunter, have only the function of acquiescence. For the interview to be a success they must misrepresent themselves. Ironically the forms, which represent an effort of almost comic earnestness to learn the truth about a person, can—as often as not—be filled out satisfactorily only if we lie. For in order to land a job most of us have to make certain false representations (or we feel that we have to). Whereas if they didn't rely on all these forms we could come across with more of the truth, the truth of *us*.

Is this another form I see before me? Not another one! No one can reasonably object to an employment form as such. It would be foolhardy for an employer to hire you without first checking your record of experience. Good enough. But what we often encounter nowadays is an overreliance on the forms, and misuse of them. There is a danger that a person may "become" his form, and be trapped inside of it.

Here are three questions on a corporation Qualification Record: "General Condition of Health; Any Serious Illness? When? Any Physical Defect or Weakness?" These inquiries are perfectly proper. But if my health were not good, I wouldn't admit it to the company. How can they expect a straight answer? I know perfectly well that a history of illness would work against my being accepted for the job, if only for actuarial reasons. Such a record might indicate that I would not live to receive my thirty-year button. On the other hand, steady employment might improve my health. But since I am dealing with a medical form, I can't say that.

The same goes for the question regarding Marital Status. There is a square provided for "Divorced." I would not care to admit that either, not because I am ashamed of it, but because, for the corporation form sheet, this is one more indication of instability. A divorced person is likely to have fewer ties than the married one; less likely to have property, such as a suburban house, to tie him down. No, it would be wiser to make good on the job and tell them about the divorce later.

The trouble is that forms crowd us so. There is no room for maneuvering one's personality around inside of them. Naturally they want to know about your previous positions, the dates, Your Position, Your Supervisor, Nature of Work, and so on. Again, well and good. But why must they ask: "Reasons for Leaving"? Who cares to answer "Fired" or "Dispute with my superior" or "Office politics"? Once more we may be forced to misrepresent the facts.

The sheet before me says: "Also account for all unemployed time since leaving school. Use additional sheet if necessary." I can't imagine any acceptable reason for being unemployed, at least for more than a few months. Honest answers might be: "Sheer incompetence, couldn't get a job," "I was inadequate," or "Working bored me." Let's say I took six months off, went to Paris, and had a lot of fun. This would indicate a most unreliable, unserious type. Again the truth is unhelpful. Give this section the rubber-band treatment—stretch your previous jobs until they almost touch, and hope that you won't be found out. It is also possible to invent jobs you have held, and alert friends to pose on the telephone as former employers. But this sort of thing is a strain on all concerned.

Some questionnaires ask you to turn informer on yourself. I remember one: "List Your Principal Weaknesses." My answer was: "None pertinent." I still don't have a clue as to what the psychologist who thought that one up considered the proper response. It seems to me that anyone who would hand his weaknesses on a platter to his future employer is a fool. Perhaps the company *doesn't* want him to admit his shortcomings, and automatically weeds out those who list them. More likely, though, he is considered cooperative and truthful. Even so, he remains a donkey who has pinned the tail on himself, for he will be hopelessly categorized from the time of his hiring.

Another technique used at many corporations is that of *simulated stress*. The idea is that you will normally encounter certain tensions on the job; therefore, why not simulate these tensions in a mild way while you are being interviewed, and see how you will react? This sounds logical enough. Here is one developed by the military during World War II to select candidates for special missions: During the interview the examiner excuses himself and leaves the room. In his absence the phone rings. Will the candidate have the initiative to answer it? And after which ring will he pick up the phone? It was found that a man's aptitude for such missions checked out closely with his readiness to lift the receiver.

I can imagine that the simulated stress method is often effective. Yet one feels an instinctive resentment against it— even if it works. A friend at the Crystal Palace, an exceptionally able man, told me a story about being courted by a large company. They paid his expenses to cross the country for an interview, and he saw that they were pleased with him. They requested that, "as a matter of form," he sit down with a psychological test. It took him about an hour to complete the questionnaire, and they asked him to wait while it was being scored.

His interviewer came back with a long face. It seemed that, amazingly enough, my friend had flunked. He couldn't imagine how it had happened. The interviewer said: "We like to be fair. Let's go through some of your answers and see what went wrong." They did, and my friend calmly justified his responses. He was about to go, when the interviewer's face lit up. "I congratulate you," he said. "We want you to come with us." He then explained that the business of flunking the test had been part of the game. It was a stress situation imposed on all candidates. My friend had in fact made a high score. "When can you start?" asked the interviewer. "Never," said my friend. "I don't want to work for anyone who cheats in the first round." Although they heaped offers on him, he didn't change his mind.

The worst thing about overreliance on forms is that, to an important extent, they can determine the course of a man's career. That is, through the medium of forms, a man may be *pursued by his past,* and his future with the company may be already indicated by his past, though he is no more than thirty-five years old.

Once, at the palace, we needed a man in our department. Someone called my superior about an applicant, and he inquired at one point: "Is that the price level he wants, or what he *is?*" The employment form asks Salary Desired. This means: "Salary to which, according to your record, you are entitled." In other words: "What salary *are* you?"

(I remember a girl explaining one reason for divorcing her husband. It was that he had "represented himself as a twelve-thousand-a-year man" when in fact he was only a seven-thousand-five-hundred-a-year man. Consequently, he had been forced to turn down several jobs paying seventy-five hundred a year in order to save face with her, and they were completely broke.)

In the corporate scheme of things, which is governed by forms, your present salary depends on your preceding one. The job that will be offered to you derives from the job you have just filled. One marches in salary fetters. Once in formation it is next to impossible to break ranks, since there is always this *form of you*, the personnel file that defines and limits your capabilities.

A Hindu conception of a man's Karma compares his lifeline and destiny to a great snake stretched over an abyss. He must eventually walk across the snake—when he dies—and each wriggle he encounters along the way represents one of the mistakes he has made. If the wriggles become too frequent and violent, he will topple off into a lower world, a lower incarnation his next time around.

In the corporate world, in a much milder way, a man's destiny is pegged out on his qualification record—before his life is one-third over. Executive Development specialists extrapolate or project his future on the basis of what he has accomplished so far, without providing for the marvelous and unexpected leaps we make, the comebacks, spurts, the discoveries, revelations, and lucky hits that come to men when their spirits roam free. The result: after years of being tabulated and boxed in, a man tends to give up his own idea of himself and *accept the evaluation from outside.* I leave it to the architects of the corporation's annual report whether to list this phenomenon under Assets (smooth-running cooperation) or Liabilities (loss of initiative and creative energy).

The employment form at the Crystal Palace asks you for: "Average Scholastic Grade from Transcript, Expressed as Percent" and "Standing in College Class." Here is another example of not being able to get the past off your back. It seems absurd to hold someone accountable for the grades he scored in his late adolescent years. Granted that they represent at least a small indicator of his competence, they also constitute a source of prejudice worse than unjust. They may turn out to be utterly misleading.

For one thing, only twenty-five per cent of us can make the first quarter of our class, and no more than fifty per cent— you might say a bare half—can look down on more people than we look up to. We don't especially mind reporting our college grades. But how about your applicants who graduated in the third and even fourth quarters? Must this ranking follow them for the rest of their lives? Wouldn't it be possible for them to go to bat without one strike on them? Find out perhaps what their grades were, but don't make these marks a part of their permanent record.

Hundreds of students every year miss the second quarter of the class by a percentage point or two. Perhaps for a good, wholesome reason. They may have been in love, or had a hangover before an important examination. They could have been sick—or their instructor may have been sick, or disappointed in love, and marked their papers savagely. Say even that the third-quarter or fourth-quarter student was unstable at that time. Say he played drums in the band and didn't study hard enough. But now it is five, ten, fifteen years later. *He is a different person now.* But on his haunting form remain the marks of his adolescence, just as though they applied today. Of course, the college record is nowhere near decisive, except for a boy twenty-one years old. At that age it may help determine his starting salary. This in turn helps fix and limit the salary he will be promoted to. True, it will be possible for him to rise above his college grades, but he will always have the house percentage—the zero and double-zero of that C— in Chemistry A on his wheel of fortune—to buck up against at promotion time.

As for the young man who has not gone to college, he is virtually untouchable so far as a middle-level job with a corporation is concerned. If Henry Ford were reincarnated he could never land a job at the Crystal Palace. In fact, on the technical side, an applicant will have quite a bit of selling to do if he can't produce a graduate school degree.

The mania for psychological testing. I have an image of a psychologist with a butterfly net pursuing the human spirit over hedges. Then, later in the laboratory, he reminds me of Marcel Marceau cradling the captive butterfly, cupping it and peering greedily at it—the difference being that Marceau's fool is heart-rendingly astonished when the life he has trapped seems dead, and he makes desperate efforts to return it to life; whereas when the investigator sees the *élan* die he does not recognize that anything has happened.

There is a principle that industrial psychologists would prefer not to live with but must. A stumbling block, it bothers them to such an extent that they are always trying to get around it—and at the same time carry on their business as if it weren't there. This is the well-known principle of indeterminancy. It tells us that a molecule (or a personality) changes simultaneously as we examine it. By turning a light on a molecule we can never, until the end of time, discover how that molecule behaves in total darkness . . . and in total darkness we can't observe it at all. Further, the warmth of the scientist's body or his heavy breathing (not to mention his non-directive questioning) may tend to produce added distortions in the molecule's behavior.[1] And if by chance he is at all clumsy with his instruments the molecule may shoot off on a tangent that departs completely from its previous pattern.

Some years ago a group of us took a test which indicates whether you are dominant or retiring in face-to-face situations. Sample question: You are waiting impatiently for a store clerk to serve you. Another customer arrives on the scene and the clerk starts to wait on him instead of you. Do you (a) remonstrate with the clerk (b) look daggers at him, but say nothing (c) leave the store? The answers have plus and minus scores, plus indicating aggressiveness and minus reporting diffidence. (In the example given, speaking sharply to the clerk represents, of course, a plus. If I remember correctly, it is less "minus" to leave the store than to remain with an injured air.)

As I say, we took this test and one of our number came out with a minus *forty-five,* which was crushingly diffident. He was exposed as a scientifically-proven Casper Milquetoast. Within a few weeks his friends became aware of a marked

---

1 Psychic researchers have maintained that a ghost would not show up at a seance if a skeptical scientist were present. But this seems a bit too easy.

change in him. He argued at the drop of a hat and reacted bitterly if anyone disagreed with him. A month later he had a fist fight in a bar, and knocked his man down. After that he was unbearable. He was always insulting people and asking them to step outside. He lost many friends, and actually became a salesman (who as a group have high plus scores in the test). In short, six months after the test you wouldn't have known him.

Again we see life imitating science. In the very act of defining my timid friend, science lost him. Suppose that the results of this test were on his record. The record would have nothing to do with him as he is *now*. It may be objected that, since his transformation was artificially induced, he is still "basically" timid. Who knows? Perhaps his diffidence was a mere overlay, and all the time he was basically aggressive. How many layers of personality are there? How many are penetrated by such questions as: "In your off-hours would you rather (a) watch a football game on TV (b) go to the ballet (c) whittle?"

Is it not possible—where people are involved—that there is a favorable time and place for scientific investigation, and also an unfavorable time? A time when investigation defeats its own ends, and becomes unfunctional? Sometimes to investigate is simultaneously to destroy. There is the story about the centipede to whom a scientist said: "Good Lord, how can you manage to walk without getting all those legs tangled up?" and the centipede became so self-conscious and embarrassed that he was tangle-footed ever after. People, of course, are very different from centipedes. Under these personality probings we tend to act more like chameleons. Investigate a young man with forms and tests to the point where he begins to imitate the form and appease the tests—

and you don't have the same young man you started out with. You had a life; now you have an imitation of life.

Another story about another friend whom I will call Nat Slocum. He was a poet who decided to go straight. For a number of years he had lived in the north woods and grown a beard, and holed up in cabins with various mistresses. One of them whom he loved brought him to a feeling of responsibility. He bought two dark suits, and shaved, and came to the city, applying for a job as an advertising copywriter. He was an attractive young man and wrote sample copy very well. The firm was delighted with his possibilities. "There's one detail," the president said, guess what, "the personality test. It's only a formality."

Nat took it, and went out to make a down payment on a Chevrolet. Two days later he returned to negotiate his starting salary. The president was embarrassed. "Nat, I'm sorry to tell you . . . it's all off."

"All off!" Nat said. "What do you mean, all off?"

"Your test . . . it shows . . . well, frankly, it comes out that you are emotionally unstable."

"Emotionally unstable!" Nat shouted. "You must be kidding! Are you out of your mind!" he roared. "What kind of a fleabag outfit is this anyway? Do you think I'd work for you!" Nat picked up his application and shredded it. "Do you see that?" he said. "That's what I think of your job!"

Concede that from the scientific point of view the test on Nat was a perfect check-out. I say to the company: you lost a fine copywriter. And you have condemned Nat forever to be a poet.

I think there are two strong arguments against massive testing: (1) More and more people are tending to accept, and worse, to seek, and worse still, to conform to outside evaluations of themselves; (2) the investigators are in danger of being swallowed up by their own techniques and machines which can only treat people as dead souls.

Ask the corporation personnel specialists why they believe so profoundly in tests and forms. The answer, as always, would seem to be eminently reasonable. Tests are designed to fit round pegs into round holes, and square pegs into square holes. Their aim is to eliminate the friction, unhappiness and inefficiency that results when an applicant is placed in the wrong job or in the wrong company. The idea is that maladjustment is bad for the individual and bad for the company; hence, why not do everything possible to avoid it? But from the standpoint of our best interests, is it necessarily a bad idea to have a square peg in a round hole? Certainly the rub produces friction, but then friction produces heat and sparks, and sometimes light. If a newcomer is uncomfortable in his job he becomes tense—nevertheless he is re-active. Something will happen, for good or ill. Assume that the job is a bit too much for him. Perhaps then he will stretch, surpass himself, become bigger sooner because of his maladjustment. Or he will fail, fold up, and have to be let go. He will in this event have *gone through the experience* of making a mistake.

Tests are aimed at depriving us of the experience of making a mistake. The assumption appears to be that it is "better" for us not to have this experience. Why is it necessarily better? Mistakes and risks build young people; profiting from mistakes makes us wiser than those who have never had a chance to be wrong. The round peg in the round hole is untested against adversity. Of course, the Crystal Palace hopes that there will never be any adversity if things are properly organized. If so, it forgets that there are always barbarians outside the walls. It forgets that complete security is a corrupting thing; that when the young people of the Palace have no chance to experience friction, tension, and selfish desire . . . and fear, the organization is going to start softening from within.

A dire symptom of this softening process is the willingness of young people to seek out tests in order to discover their aptitudes. Let's say the findings are right, the tests are right. Taking them may still be wrong, again, because *you* haven't done the work of self-discovery; *they* have done the work. The tests are also assuming a static you, as-you-are-now. They gauge your potential, yes. But achievement involves the interaction of potential and challenge. "I didn't know I had it in me" is the expression. Well, it is possible that the tests don't know either.

I remember a girl who took a series of tests to discover her aptitudes. To her consternation, she learned that she had a moderate and equal aptitude for everything. Shortly afterward she gave herself in marriage and now, ten years later, has five children.

The wisdom of Pascal:

"People are generally better persuaded by the reasons they have themselves discovered than by those which have come into the minds of others."

Also:

"The greater intellect one has, the more originality one finds in men. Ordinary persons find no difference between men."

The more tabulating machines are used to measure people, the farther we are from knowing one another. What kind of machines measure us? Consider, for example, the Interaction Chronograph.

The inventor of this device is anthropologist Eliot D. Chapple. For some years he has been noted for his observations and measurements of organizational behavior, among other places, in large companies. His techniques have been used in selecting new personnel for these companies; they have also been tested extensively on mental patients.

Mr. Chapple adopts the anthropological approach to organization, viewing it as a system of relations between people. In an article, "The Man, The Job, and the Organization," appearing in the March-April 1958 number of *Personnel*, a magazine published by the American Management Association, he and Leonard R. Sayles ask: "But how can we go about matching people and the organization to each other?"

They outline this method:

"The key to our approach lies in the question, what do we look at? The answer is that we observe how people behave with one another *on the job,* their interaction in the daily routine of activities in the company. By watching an executive and the way he spends his time, we can immediately make a number of helpful distinctions. We can observe the difference between how much time he spends in contact with other people and which other people. We can see that while he initiates some contacts, others are initiated to him. We can observe his relationship with his boss, or the department head who precedes him in the work flow. We can make many objective notes about how he reacts to these differing personalities."

I reread this paragraph with growing wonder. It was not that I questioned the authors' premises. Something else . . . I went on to another paragraph:

"We can measure each man's contacts on the job in order to describe how he behaves with different people; from these measurements, we can then prepare a job description which—unlike those commonly employed in industry today—tells us when an executive is to act, with whom, and for how long; we can even employ interaction measurement as a selection and placement tool."

There follows this extended footnote which I will let speak for itself, except that the italics are mine:

"2 Though all this could be done by *a group of observers with stopwatches*, it is far more efficient to record the interaction directly into a computer, called the Interaction Chronograph, which processes the measurements into manageable form. The Interaction Chronograph provides a technical means of measuring personality traits and temperamental reactions. In selection and placement, a standardized interview is employed in which the interviewer simulates the crucial interaction situations which occur in our daily contacts. By controlling the length and timing of the interviewer's acts, we can measure how the interviewee *reacts to the stress of not obtaining a response* or being subjected to opposition or competition and what kind of reaction, if any, he shows after each type of stress is over. . . ."

Now for the Interaction Chronograph itself. The workings of Mr. Chapple's instrument have been described in the *Journal of Psychology*.[2] It began as "a moving tape, driven at uniform speed, upon which lines were drawn continuously when the keys were pressed down." These lines in effect scored the test conversations. The research paper explains:

2 For reference see "The Interaction Chronograph As An Instrument For Objective Measurement of Interaction Patterns During Interviews" by Joseph D. Matarazzo, George Saslow, and Ruth G. Matarazzo, Massachusetts General Hospital and Harvard Medical School, published in the *Journal of Psychology*, Vol. 41 (1956). This study was supported by a research grant from the National Institute of Mental Health.

"With this innovation Chapple could measure not only the length of time each person talked or acted (his action) and the length of time he was silent (silence variable), obtaining a continuous record of this sequence of action and silence, he could also record variation in the adjustment of the participants to each other. The record indicates who interrupted, how long the interruption lasted, which one dominated by talking the other down. Further, if there was a silence during which one person failed to respond to the other, the record indicated who was responsible for the silence, how long the silence lasted (i.e. who was failing to 'adjust' and how long this failure of adjustment lasted) and who finally *initiated* the next action."

I would like to inject one mild dissent here. I have a friend who dominates people and conversations by his aggressive silence. He simply looks at the victim and says: "Uh huh" or "Yes?", or frowns, and the other continues wildly trying to explain himself. On the Interaction Chronograph, it seems to me, the lines might seem to represent one person haranguing or dominating another, whereas he is actually pleading to be understood by the dominant one.

The paper tells how the Interaction Chronograph has recently been modernized.

"Chapple developed a computer which would draw cumulative curves of interaction patterns while these were being recorded by the observer; i.e. much as Skinner's animals have always plotted their own learning curves. (The new model) consists of two parts; a small observer's box and a large recording machine, with which the former is connected by a long, flexible cable, thus providing for the possibility of the two parts being housed in different rooms . . . The observer's box has five keys or buttons which are operated manually by the observer while the interview is in progress."

The keys on Mr. Chapple's panel are fascinating in themselves, but without going into detail it is enough to report here that by arithmetic combinations of the variables they produce he can determine such characteristics of job applicants as "pretentiousness," "emotionality," "ability to take the floor," and "shyness." With a machine, he can do this!

What lies behind it all? The authors of the research paper say:

"He (Chapple) has taken the position that personality can be assessed without recourse to intra-psychic and other currently popular psychodynamic formulations, and further that this assessment involves merely the process of observing the *time relations* in the interaction patterns of people. Accordingly, Chapple has indicated that this method, because of its objectivity, can lead to a science of personality."

Here, once more, we meet the fetish of "objective observation" now being applied in the relations between man and man. It gives rise to such rather startling observations as this:

"However . . . experience has indicated that 'the interviewer' is not an objective scientific instrument. . . ."

and

"It will be apparent from the discussion so far that the observer is an important person in the conduct of research with the Interaction Chronograph since he is, in effect, part of the instrument."

Mr. Chapple's measurement of people in terms of time elements may, for all the layman knows, be perfectly valid. But it seems to me that the off-stage measurement of men and women (by means of a hidden observer of one kind or another) while they are on a job or applying for one demonstrates in itself a stunning moral misunderstanding of what life is all about.

All such methods assume that it is morally defensible for *somebody to be listening to us* from behind a curtain or a wall, plotting the curves of our reactions as though an employee or a job hunter, a private citizen in his right mind, were a laboratory mouse. The applicant is tested and categorized without permission, without his being aware of it. He thinks he is talking across the desk to a person, but in fact he is talking to a machine. This private citizen is to all intents and purposes being wiretapped while he is looking for a job.

Wouldn't the eavesdropping Polonius be surprised if, some day, an outraged candidate detected the rustling of the drapes, leaped up from his chair and seized the interviewer's letter opener, shouted: "How now! A rat? Dead, for a ducat, dead!" and stabbed him through the curtain? That would show initiative; I would hire such a man.

The proper question is not so much whether these various questionnaires, tests, faked interviews, etc. *work* as selection and placement tools. For the sake of argument, let's suppose that some of them do. We may still ask: "Who needs them?" Is it necessary or even desirable to be absolutely exact about someone's capacity? To arrive at this supposed exactitude, industry becomes a spying world. With the best of motives, we condone an invasion of privacy by trickery.

I wonder, too, whether all this investigative apparatus is

not somewhat too expensive. The company maintains a substantial employee-relations group to process people. The supposition is that what we have called intuitive methods of hiring are in the long run more expensive than the testing apparatus. Maybe this isn't true at all. At the Crystal Palace, thank heaven, hiring is not done by instruments. But our personnel specialists cost a great deal of money. Employee Relations is a big, unwieldy department, one of the largest in the company. Fewer "relations" might make for rougher hiring and firing processes. But over the years administrative costs might be less if the department were cut down.

Finally, may we not trust a sensitive personnel man to judge the qualifications of a candidate without the aid of costly scientific props—to employ judgment rather than measurement? Let him rely on his own free perceptions. Surely they will be wrong on occasion, but that won't mean the end of the world for either the applicant or the corporation.

We are in love with systems, yet often it turns out that they are not as sacrosanct as we pretend. It is probably not fair to bring this up, but, for instance, the Crystal Palace is filled with nephews and nieces. What psychology is used in hiring them?

And who *are* the systematic, scientific gods that receive our obeisance? Perhaps they are not gods at all, but on the contrary rather unhappy and ill-adjusted men. What kind of person enjoys measuring the characters of others? Just as a guess, I would bet that the enthusiasts of measurement have fewer friends than most of us do. This bet would be made on the premise that those who seek to trap and tabulate the inner impulses of others, particularly by deception, have a basic contempt for these same impulses. (I realize that, scientifically, this is a foolish thought. How do we define "friendship"?, etc.) He who thinks your self is capturable by machine must proceed from a basic (if perhaps kindly) contempt for you—seldom a starting point for friendliness.

I once heard a strong and good personnel man whose proper advancement had been held back by upstairs stupidity trying to account for his slow progress. He complained for a while about certain inefficiencies. But obviously he felt that his grousing wasn't getting to the heart of the matter. Then he burst out: "I know I have faults, and they're serious! They have hurt me. I'm too impatient. I let my personal feelings get the better of me! I try to control them—but when I'm not thinking they come out!"

This was his confession to the gods of personnel. He spoke loudly, as though he hoped to be overheard, to assure the powers of what-is-right that he was not vain. And this *mea culpa* was bunk. He had none of these faults. He was a good man precisely because on occasion he let his personal feelings get the better of him.

The curious self-denunciations we hear nowadays! The tyranny of forms has produced a new type of confessional. Instead of (or in addition to) confessing to God through his priest, or confessing to himself via a psychoanalyst, the corporation man confesses to the Form. He acknowledges his strengths and weaknesses as they have been defined by others, and promises in his subdued heart to do better, to con to the form, or at least to appear to do so. And if you appear to think in a certain way for twenty years, the chances are that somewhere along the line you will be absorbed into your own disguise.

To advance carefully within the Form is the one and only secret of success in the Crystal Palace.

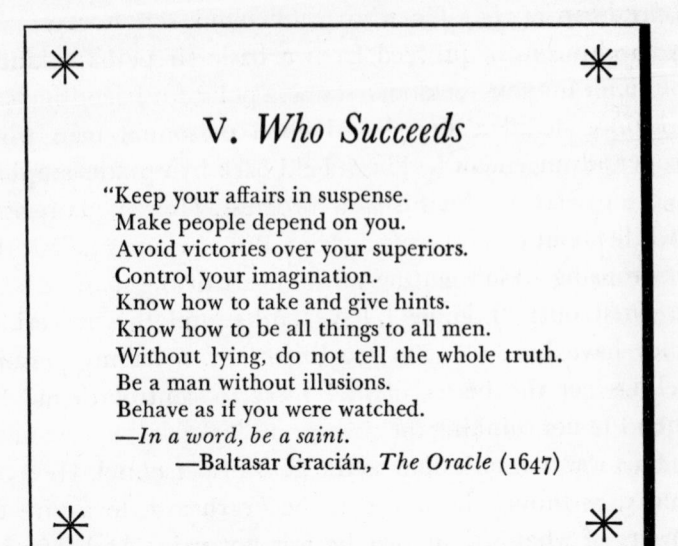

V. *Who Succeeds*

"Keep your affairs in suspense.
Make people depend on you.
Avoid victories over your superiors.
Control your imagination.
Know how to take and give hints.
Know how to be all things to all men.
Without lying, do not tell the whole truth.
Be a man without illusions.
Behave as if you were watched.
—*In a word, be a saint.*
—Baltasar Gracián, *The Oracle* (1647)

Rules for getting ahead don't change very much through the centuries. Baltasar Gracián knew nothing of corporations, yet his advice could be tacked up on the wall of every office in the Crystal Palace. This Jesuit writer understood power. He observed the techniques of advancement as they were practiced in the great organizations of court and church in Spain. The same trusty methods, with a few modifications, hold good in our own courts of industry.

A warning here: since the Year One writers have been disclosing the secrets of achieving and holding power within an organization. But with rare exceptions, *they* have seldom wielded important executive power. It may be that they talk too much. The rulers of a province or a business are generally not too fond of articulate professionals. Machiavelli never held a big job. Gangsters despise their mouthpieces. In the times of the robber barons the effete chap who could read and push the quill was not greatly admired. The scribe of chivalric times and the corporation ghost writer have about the same status and function—to celebrate the activities of the doers. These tame chroniclers of court and company histories are nevertheless distrusted, for words are the enemy of power.

Despised by the men of action, the scribes are sometimes found allied in intrigues to get back at them. It should always be remembered that writers detest the power of others. Yet business success has held an often fatal fascination for scribes. How, they wonder, is it possible for these unlettered dolts to make money and hold important positions when I can't? Bankruptcy records yield the names of writers, like Balzac and Mark Twain, who seemed to understand business perfectly but lost their shirts in commercial ventures of their own. It appears that the people who are successful in commerce can't put into words (or don't care to let on) exactly how they do it. Therefore, it is left to the envious scribe to explain it for them.

What then is the touchstone of success for the corporation man? Are the tactics different from those you would use in smaller enterprises? I have heard many theories. After several years of watching (and having attained a sort of middle-junior executive rank), I have compiled a few tentative conclusions.

Begin with a rough list of successful business types. I offer these: (1) the freebooter (2) the operator (3) the administrator or "official" (4) the professional. Then there are subcategories: (a) the adviser or consultant (vizier, gray eminence) (b) the efficiency man (c) the court favorite (d) the scribe (public relations) (e) the entertainer.

Taking the major categories in order, we have no free-booters in our company. Men like Mike Todd would go out of their minds at the Palace. We know the freebooter. His operations are speculative and personal. Assuming that he has capital, he swings life by the tail. Lacking capital, he charms, tricks, or bulldozes others into going along with him. What he does thereafter is his own business, not ours. We are talking about success *within* organizations. The free-booter is always on his own, or on top, or he is nothing.

We know the operator, too, but curiously enough we may not recognize him when he operates on *us*. He is a connois-seur of vanity and weakness. To borrow a phrase from sport, he remains at all times "well within himself." This person seeks domain, the next highest position, the neighboring tract of land. He probes for soft spots either in you or in the situation immediately confronting him. His guiding princi-ple is to exert leverage in order to unblock obstacles without seeming to do so. There are all kinds of leverage—your weakness, a personality clash in which he serves as an honest broker, doing his superior's homework and thereby making himself indispensable, covertly encouraging quarrels between others, filling vacuums in the organization, obtaining scarce theater tickets, etc.

Operators are not necessarily bad people. Most of us op-erate on occasion. That is, we subtly call attention to our-selves, go out of our way to be agreeable, and try to occupy corners of knowledge so that the ones in power can't easily do without us. If the source of power enjoys burlesque shows, we may take him to a burlesque show with no harm done. Good operators know their limitations, and proceed carefully from one limited objective to the next. Almost inevitably, if he is effective, the operator will oust someone or push ahead of him, and that is why he is disliked. On the other hand, disliked or not, he usually survives.

It seems to me that there are relatively fair and unfair ways of operating. We might say that a fair operator tries to get ahead without injuring others too much, while the conniver will tunnel under his rivals' positions with the relentlessness of a mole. Here are three operators:

A soldier I knew during World War II didn't care to go overseas. He became the headquarters' chief file clerk and built a filing system of his own so that nobody else could find anything. Every time his name came up for overseas duty he spoke earnestly of "reorganizing the files." But the more he reorganized them the more complicated they became. He could locate all required papers in an instant; when he went on furlough headquarters was a bedlam. The end of the war found him still on the job and, within a few months, home free.

An assistant promotion manager had not the least suspicion that his boss' new secretary was out to supplant him. She was a motherly woman of thirty-five and soon divined that the boss was a bit of a mamma's boy. She ran personal errands and brought him warm milk, and when his cigarette lighter would not work she fixed it. The boss, she discovered, did not particularly like the assistant manager but was awed by his intellect. The secretary therefore looked up a number of words in the dictionary that are often wrongly defined (one was "livid") and artfully led the conversation around to them. After escaping several traps (although he had no idea that they were traps) the assistant manager fell into two wrong definitions. In front of the boss, she triumphantly produced Webster's. Since the assistant manager was an emotional person he made the mistake of arguing and turned himself into a fool. Thereafter, she kept questioning his vocabulary. He flew into one or two embarrassing rages and, generally undermined, started sulking. He was fired, and she took over his position.

There were two rival assistant managers in a company. One was a direct-action man. The other, who had risen above a timid disposition, was a subtler thinker than his extroverted opponent. It was the stiletto versus the meat ax. There came a day when the two were to present conflicting courses of action to the firm's directors. It was clear that the man who put across the winning program would be promoted over the other. The big-fisted assistant manager knew that his rival, a bachelor, was sensitive and finicky about sexual matters. As they confronted one another at the crucial meeting, he suddenly roared at him, making a huge, appropriate gesture: "All right! You put your premise on the table and I'll put my premise on the table, and we'll see which is longer!" This onslaught so upset the timid one that he floundered and flubbed his presentation. "And now," smiles Sales Manager Number One, "he's getting used to the idea of working for me."

At the Crystal Palace our operators are nowhere near so violent. Strictly speaking, we do not have any full-time operators. Rules and procedures are so carefully laid out, and seniority is so well protected, that it becomes nearly impossible for a lone wolf to oust anyone. Further, since decisions are made by committee, only small portions of credit or blame can be assigned to one person. Under these conditions, operating has evolved into a most gentlemanly, long, long-term affair. It would be safe to say that every up-and-coming executive operates a little bit, but his scope is limited. He must confine himself to small ingratiations and modest **advances**. Operating in this fashion may be considered *de rigeur* in a large company. Such tactics will work; they always do. But since they are carried out in a restrained and gentlemanly fashion, they cannot be compared with the methods of the classic tunnel artist.

At the Crystal Palace, it should be emphasized, maneuverings of this kind are only frosting on the cake. In general, the successful corporation man is the one who can prove through the years that he is a good administrator. "Administration" is the key. The man, and to a lesser extent, the woman who knows how to use it will unlock the doors, one by one, that lead to the top floor.

Along with the administrator goes the professional, who seldom rises as high. The relationship between these two groups is interesting. Administrator and professional apparently cannot exist without one another, and yet they are by nature mutually hostile. The administrators organize the work of professionals; whereas the professionals *do* all the work. The administrator or "official" is primarily interested in obtaining a smooth work flow in accordance with regulations. The professional's main concern is with excellent performance of a particular job.

The official wants to maintain a department that *seems* efficient; the specialist aches to *be* efficient. A great many corporation executives begin as specialists, and then, if they are rated outstanding, are promoted to an administrative position. Yet the specialist-turned-administrator may well prove to be less effective than one of those talentless desk men, the born "officials," the defenders of bottlenecks, who have filled table-of-organization squares since the dawn of time. That is because the specialist tends to overemphasize the importance of his own profession in the larger picture—and an enterprise of any size involves an effort of combined professions. In contrast, the official in the classic mould is not hampered by a belief in anything but rules, procedures, and rank.

In *Dead Souls,* Gogol takes us to an official-type provincial party in early nineteenth-century Russia:

"The men here as everywhere were of two kinds; the thin who were always hanging about the ladies and . . . the stout (who) looked askance at the ladies and held aloof from them, while they gazed about to see whether the governor's servants had yet set the table for whist. . . . These were the more dignified officials of the town. Alas! The stout know better how to manage their affairs than the thin. The thin serve rather on special commissions or are mere supernumeraries, sent here and there. Their existence is somehow too light and airy and not to be depended upon. The stout never go by by-paths but always keep on the main road, and if they seat themselves anywhere they sit firmly and reliably so that their seat is more likely to give way under them than they are to be dislodged from it."

It is the same today—the successful administrator plumps himself down firmly and reliably. He sits at an office crossroads, across lines of communication. He throws switches. If he were not on the job, presumably, trains would run into each other. He has a veto power over trains of thought, and may keep them on a siding indefinitely, or even derail them if he thinks they are going too fast.

This describes his position, but not what he does. For years three questions have disturbed me. What *is* an administrator? What on earth is his talent? And why are people like me always working for people like him?

I am in my office at the Crystal Palace writing a speech for one of the directors. He has, of course, virtually no idea what he is going to say until I show it to him. Not that he couldn't work up a speech that would be perfectly satisfactory, but he hasn't time for words. Outside, a maintenance worker is maneuvering his power mower across our superb front lawn. I hear a slapping sound—the window washer leaning back against his strap douses the glass before my eyes, washing out my view of the lawn mower. I return to my typing and the phone rings. I am called into the administrator's office for consultation.

What is this executive doing? He stands at his desk holding a piece of paper. He frowns. Several professionals gather around him. When we have all arrived he advises us that a group of town officials wish to tour our plant. We must greet them in a certain way. He calls for suggestions. Everybody puts in a word. He says, all right, Joe will do this, Jim will do that, and Bob will do the other by next Wednesday. At this point there is a soft crash and spray of foam against the window pane, and the muffled thrumming of the power mower immediately below the window. The administrator smiles and says: "Men working . . . well, let's adjourn," and our consultation is over.

The meeting has lasted for ten minutes. It suddenly occurs to me that during this period our superior, the official, hasn't done any work. He didn't propose anything; he only listened to our proposals. He isn't going to do anything; we are carrying out the assignments. He simply heard us out and distributed the jobs. The man hanging on the strap was doing something; there are no specks on our windows. The lawn mower made the grounds prettier. I will type something (less useful) that will give the town officials a better idea of the plant. But he, this one, who is always *standing there* or *sitting there* holding that eternal piece of paper, makes twice as much money as I do, and four times as much as the washer and mower.

Work, basically, involves lifting something. I "lift my hand" to a project, or lift ideas out of my mind. The official lifts only his hat—to the people who matter. Yet he is incredibly more successful than the professionals who work under him, because he "sees to it" that we do our jobs. One can understand that. He is arranging, channeling, disposing, traveling, consulting. The only thing he does not do is produce.

One day I took a random look through the files of our administrative correspondence. The letters: announced the availability of some booklets; asked the opinion of higher authority on possible contributions to a fund; advised that a film be shown to a certain group; replied to a school teacher's request for booklets; informed higher authority of this request and listed the booklets sent to the teacher; sent background material on the company to an advertising agency; requested higher authority's approval of an editorial to be run in the house organ: "Are we on sound ground as far as the general image we should be trying to convey to our people?"; explained to lower authority the uses of a kit, and commented on the plans of a branch office. . . .

This is administration, and it is fine. No company could function without it. The question in my mind is not why corporate administrators exist (someone has to expedite things) but why they are so well paid. After watching scores of them in action, I could swear that their duties consist mainly of *frowning* over sheets of paper, consulting with others, and then passing on the job-to-be-done to a specialist.

Yet the fact is that they are highly paid, and always have been, and they usually do surpass their professional opposite numbers in rank and salary, and always have—therefore, there must be some enduring reason for their success. The typical official can't build a bridge or construct a machine, or plant an original idea about anything. But those that plant them are soon forgotten. He must know something. I believe the administrator possesses these important abilities:

1. He has the talents of a cork. There are great advantages in being an intellectual lightweight. The professional man will sink or swim with his ideas. He takes chances. The official, having no ideas to burden him, can bob around like a buoy or marker in the roughest water while others are dashed against the rocks.

2. The absence of creative ability is a talent in itself. In a corporation it can be a positive asset. It gives the pure executive a broader view of any problem than the specialist will have. The designer of a bridge, for instance, visualizes a span that will be beautifully constructed, let it be with expensive materials, to last hundreds of years. The bridge is everything to him. He will probably, if given his way, spend too much money on it. But the bridge, as the official well knows, is not everything to the corporation. It may be one of many expensive undertakings, and there is just so much money available.

The administrator has only a passing interest in beauty. He is not limited by an aesthetic sense. He is immune to the specialist's pain, the pain of caring. He cares only about the organization and orders from above. Hence, he remains utterly free to firm up, facilitate, and finalize without any qualms. He explains to the architect in kindly fashion that the bridge cannot be ornamented with gargoyles, even if it would violate the entire conception of the structure not to have them, because "upstairs they have taken a negative attitude on that." The architect's wails will not move him. But then if it turns out overnight that the board chairman's wife likes gargoyles after all, the official will happily pass on the good word to the specialist. Observe that no matter how many times the decision is changed the man without ideas remains unaffected, while the creative man's standing fluctuates up and down.

3. A good administrator has a remarkable talent for staying out of trouble. A prominent adviser to corporations tells me that Rule Number One for the ambitious executive is never to identify himself emotionally with a project. If the venture should fail he becomes too easy a target. If it succeeds he becomes a marked man; in other words, a number of people will be hoping that he fails next time. Further, to take an emotional stand may involve antagonizing somebody. This is all right for a professionally talented person, but if your ability is purely administrative what is the good of getting anyone mad at you?

To avoid blame, the corporation bureaucrat always goes by the book. He memorizes handbooks, code books, and rule books. He worships proper procedure and mortally fears anyone who creates a situation not covered by the book. The book is a covenant worked out by mediocre people to frustrate outlaws. The outlaw is the original man. Originality produces disorder and change. Hence, it must be controlled by procedure. Only through procedure can slow imaginations throw a halter over minds that would otherwise bolt ahead of the group.

4. The pure executive is also adept, generally in a nice way, at credit-grabbing. Nor does he have to work very hard at it. The corporate apparatus is so rigged that the administrator who has merely distributed jobs can take a share of credit for their execution. For the specialists have been cor-

raled into a team of which he is the captain. All correspondence reads in effect: *"We* have done such-and-such . . ."
This implies participation of the official when in fact he may
have done absolutely nothing. I recall an editorial supervisor reporting to his boss on a particularly good story: "Stan
Richards did the leg work on that." The fact was that Richards had done *all* of the story, not only the leg work but the
head work and the writing. The supervisor's contribution
was exactly zero. But in the act of seeming to praise him,
this official managed to indicate that his subordinate had
played a relatively minor role.

5. Successful bureaucrats have a form of intelligence that
specialists often lack. Again it is a centuries-old faculty that
can't be dismissed: *they keep their eyes on the ball.* This
sounds easy, but most of us don't do it. At least we don't at
all times.

We see Gogol's thin men at the governor's party wasting
their time with the ladies. Their eyes are off the ball. The
ball is the governor. Or more immediately, the ball is the
official who stands one rung higher than you. The stout men
strike us as pompous and foolish in their stuffy observances of
procedure. The affair itself is a caricature waiting for the
satirist to come along.

But does the satirist understand life any better than the
fat men? Do I know life any better than the administrators
at the Crystal Palace who hire me to ghostwrite their speeches?
Perhaps the buxom official knows what he, with his modest
talents, must do in order to advance. The high-spirited satirist laughs at him—but one day the scoffer will be writing wise
and witty speeches for this official . . . and the official will
be applauded as a statesman. Who is the ventriloquist and
who the dummy?

You will notice in administrators on the way up a certain

fixed, calculating expression, and nothing moves it out of their eyes. This means that our executive is on the ball. Satire to him is the play of children; irreverent humor is stupid; whatever lies outside the book does not concern him. He is oriented wholly toward power. He will give you his courteous exterior, the friendly smile and offhand joke, but his eye remains fixed on that one spot—where the power is.

6. Finally, the pure official understands the relative value of things and the relative importance of people. This is sometimes called "judgment." It is supposed to improve with experience, and probably does.

The official has also managed to foist on the world the fetish of "experience." This has been quite an achievement because in many kinds of work it doesn't mean very much. "The value of experience" is a concept frequently used by old men to keep young men down. For example, at the time of the Suez crisis in 1956 it was pointed out with absolute authority by old hands that the Egyptian pilots and their recruited foreign colleagues "lacked the experience" to move ships through the Canal's tricky currents. This turned out to be nonsense.

I suspect that most jobs in a corporation and elsewhere can be mastered in a few months, or at any rate in a year or two. What cannot be learned that quickly is the corporation minuet—the respectful dance with the right partners. The watchful corporation man gradually finds out who is important and who is not; what is acceptable and what is not; what type of project will advance his fortunes and what is not worth bothering about. Experience for him mainly adds up to learning how to behave. The secrets of gaging and responding to the power of others—superimposed on a normal intelligence—will move him slowly upward.

The process involves no great wear and tear. In this way, if you wish, you may become one of those men whom Caesar liked to have around him—"sleek-headed men, and such as sleep o' nights." There are worse fates, by far.

To be able to sleep at night, isn't that important? Not all successful people can sleep, or let you sleep. There are the tyrants, the maniacs, the lashing, driving executives for whom work is a disease. They give a continuous and monstrous devotion to the labors of business . . . at the expense of their own humanity and, often, the human rights of others.

This is not to suggest that the hardest sort of work and devotion to a cause are in any way abnormal. Rather we are talking about someone who worships work-in-itself, who perhaps uses the job as an opiate to help him forget people. Watch out when a man's work becomes more important than its objective; when he disappears into his duties.

The maniac who does not really believe that others exist, except as a part of his dream, is, classically, an idealist—a dweller in the realm of Idea. This idea may be Production or Efficiency or Money or Success. But he does not relate these things to the enjoyment of life. They are ends in themselves. Nothing else matters to him. He defines himself in terms of process; he becomes a process that walks like a man.

An individual of this sort, we know, both succeeds and fails. He succeeds in that his contributions to industry may be enormous—or, if enormously trivial, still in their small frame impressive. (A demoniacal executive may expend as much energy as Napoleon in carrying out a promotion campaign to boost the sales of, say, horse meat.) He fails in that his life or the lives around him are made miserable.

There is nothing new in this. We flail away at old sins with no real hope of change. Yet change gradually has produced . . . the Crystal Palace. For at our company we have all but done away with tyrants. Whatever its faults, the corporation has demonstrated for all to see a decent collective respect for human dignity. The mediocre man's protective league may stifle initiative, but it also has a civilized conscience and a good heart. The Crystal Palace has no use for pagan executives. It has shown that a business society can get along without maniacs, even if the maniacs are super-productive.

Those who are eaten up by work need not be tyrants. Some are little people, such as office girls and clerks, or gloomy, withdrawn desk men who injure no one but themselves. It is hard to forget the obsessed men and women I have met in business. Perversely, I rather miss them, and yet it is a relief to know that they are employed in another part of the forest. I wonder whether corporation life offers the cure for what ails them, or whether they suffer from a scourge that will lash them anywhere. Probably they will suffer and make us suffer, no matter what the environment.

I remember ten years ago a top-level executive in a corporation served by our public relations agency. The first thing to be said about Thomas MacKenzie, as I will call him, is that he worked absolutely all the time, Saturdays, Sundays, holidays, during lunch hour, and in his chauffeur-driven limousine. He consumed his job as though it were food. He was once interviewed on the radio, and this exchange took place:

Interviewer: "Please tell us about your hobbies."

MacKenzie: "Work is my only hobby. The only thing that interests me is working. That, you can say, will be my hobby for the rest of my life."

The interviewer was politely incredulous. One can imagine his nervous smile as he tried to extract a semblance of human interest from this sub-captain of industry. He prodded: "Come now, Mr. MacKenzie, no other hobby?" There was none. Finally, I am sure in response to a nudge or gesture from the near-by public-relations attendant, the dragon muttered something about golf and cribbage, but it was obvious that he couldn't care less about these pastimes or any other.

I remember him during one of those civil defense air-raid alerts that send everyone scurrying to the basement. These affairs are no respecters of rank. The directors and high administrators come down from the upper floors and jam in with everybody else until the all-clear, which, on this day when our agency people were guests in their shelter, they did with smiles and democratic friendliness. But not Tom MacKenzie. Plainly he was outraged by this intrusion on his time and by the corporate rabble that surrounded him.

He looked neither to the left nor right, but stared directly ahead of him at a post, sucking on a cigarette, moving the butt rhythmically into and out of his mouth like a mechanical smoking-man in a drug-store window. His drawn, oddly boyish face expressed only a determination to endure this dreadful interlude. After a few minutes the atmosphere became close and he gasped for air, and then the all-clear bell sounded.

He smoked at least four packs of cigarettes a day, sipping, sipping at them, never inhaling. At a lengthy meeting in which movies were being shown, a junior executive heard

MacKenzie's hoarse voice beside him asking for a cigarette. Hastily obliging, he laid the pack on a chair between them. A half-hour later he reached for a cigarette, and found that they were all gone, and the pack crumpled, and saw, still two seats away, MacKenzie imperturbably smoking.

MacKenzie's greatest asset, apart from his devotion to work, was impatience. He would not put up with the most reasonable excuse for a job not being done. He appeared to regard company employees now as ten pins with faces painted on them, and again as human furniture that was always in need of rearrangement. I believe he thought that ideas were alive and had to be moved through people, who were inanimate.

This man conducted a raging counterpoint across the corporation's gentlemanly routine. He despised idleness and detected signs of it in every glass-walled office. When he gave orders, people tumbled and jumped, and stayed late, and the girls sometimes burst into tears. For this reason he preferred male help around him. Married, he was seldom at home. His home was his brief case.

At an advanced age he cut out from business, obtained an economics degree, and then returned to the company. It goes without saying that MacKenzie was inexhaustible. He always had been, since his days as a boy on a western ranch when he walked four miles to school, and later sold vacuum cleaners to finance himself through college.

He had a ferocious sense of protocol and privilege, and in a strange way he could be corrupt. Caprice was his corruption. In his younger days he had served for a few years in one of the corporation's difficult territories. This stint did not last long, and thereafter he gravitated to headquarters and stayed there. Nevertheless he developed a headlong prejudice in favor of employees who had served in that same difficult territory. Men were abruptly promoted and favored in many ways simply because they worked in the area where he had his early experience.

MacKenzie, the fierce perfectionist, was a huge roadblock in the way of hiring new personnel for important jobs. Above a certain salary bracket, they all had to pass his scrutiny, and he almost never found them suitable. That was because, again, he felt that jobs were alive and people were figurines. He considered each job a child of his whom no one was good enough to marry.

I have heard from several sources that our man was, curiously enough, a physical coward. If so, I am sure that the main reason was his disdain for the physical proximity of others. The idea of anyone laying hands on him would have made him physically ill. Yet I am convinced that MacKenzie would only have been made impatient by the imminence of his own death. He would have rejected last rites in order to have more time for dictation. This was his virtue as well as his disaster. Permitting no sham or flim-flam from others, he nevertheless led a shammed life. He had a home; he must have been loved, but he conveyed an impression of loneliness. His lonely walks to school dissolved to splendid, solitary rides in a limousine from his estate to the city. Coming up the front steps he turned neither to the left nor right, and acknowledged no one. Somewhere along the way he parted company with the rest of us.

In an elevator I heard two men discussing an acquaintance who had come down with a violent attack of gout. One said: "Well, to sandwich your lunch between six gin-and-tonics and five coronas is pretty ridiculous." Well, yes. Pity the maniac who systematically abuses his body. We had one like that some years ago in the advertising agency.

Edwin Kern meant no harm, but in the office he was felt to

be an abomination. He had brought a difficult account to the firm and managed it in a style best described as hysterical. Possibly this was the one way it could be handled, since the client was a diamond-studded bastard who appeared to equate service with pain. Only if the account executive suffered were the client's representatives convinced that a good job was being done. I don't think they were especially cruel by nature; it was just that pain was the most accurate measurement they knew.

At any rate, the two parties sought each other out and were a perfect fit. Kern was a masochistic maniac—the only one I have ever seen. He came to life when he was imposed upon, and could pass the imposition on to others, so that we would all groan together in his misery. Every time he came down the hall in an urgent trot it was sure to be bad news. At the last minute the client had rejected a piece of copy or art work. There would have to be a meeting on Friday night. The client had turned thumbs down on an entire series, and it would be necessary to come up with new roughs by Monday morning.

He would wring his hands, clutch his temples and plead with us. He would threaten at one moment, and then all but go down on his knees the next. He was fat and forty-five. He had a frighteningly swollen white face, and dyed his hair black. When he became emotional, which could happen at any time, his cheeks would tremble and his eyes would seem to bulge out in terror. He spoke in a husky voice that would sink into the whisper of a damned man whenever he was thwarted.

Kern had a male secretary. (No girl could have survived a week of these maddening hysterics.) The young man loathed and constantly insulted him. He didn't seem to mind. You could say anything you wanted to him. You would be overwhelmed in the end by this flabby crybaby, spoil your weekend and ruin your digestion, to save his job for him. I never understood at the time why we did give in, but we always did. Now I think I know. We were in the presence of a tearful tyrant who, for all his chewing of the scenery, didn't believe in our existence. Short of killing him, there was no way to get rid of him. He once followed a production assistant all the way to the railroad station pleading for help until the man turned around and came back to the office. Thus, if we don't have a strong enough dream of our own, we conform to, and become a character in, the obsessed man's dream.

I look back on a picture of Kern in one of his characteristic agonies. There was, of course, a last-minute change. The client was on one phone and the engraver on another. Both were outraged. Kern was sitting between two desks, straining to bring the phones together, but the cords weren't long enough, so that his arms were hung out as though he were on a rack. He couldn't bring his mouth close to the speaker of either phone without dropping the other, which he didn't dare do. He was reduced to bellowing, transmitting messages back and forth between the two phones, in which remote voices were buzzing on and on no matter what he said.

I left for the army, and later heard that Kern had suffered a heart attack. He was slowly getting well in the hospital when he insisted on making a few business calls. In the middle of a conversation with the client he fell dead.

There are girls, too, with a mania for extra labor, but theirs is almost always defensive. It represents a shutting out of life and finding peace in the opiate of paper work. Or perhaps it is like playing with dolls on lonely weekday evenings and Saturday afternoons with one light burning over the desk, and all around, the dark, peaceful sanctuary of the deserted office.

I can see Frances Burkhardt with whom I worked before going to the Palace staggering into the office on Monday mornings in a state of, sad to say, comic exhaustion as a result of her weekend labors amid piles of correspondence. Her charming little Punch-and-Judy face would be all pale and hollowed out under the eyes. She blinked at everyone, and could hardly see across the room. All the work was unnecessary, of course. It seemed comic to us because Frances was running away from a rich boy friend who wanted to marry her. She was funny, in a sweet way, like a blushing maiden embracing paper and more paper to escape a worse sacrifice. But she gave in, and was married, and her affair with the filing cabinets ended.

Turning the situation around, one's heart goes out to girls who are married to work maniacs. True, they don't have to worry so much about money. Such men are probably going to be good providers of what money can buy. What they frequently do not provide in the home is their presence in it. Strange men, who can't bring themselves to go home when the sun sets!

I worked in a real-estate office where we had not one but eight of these barbarians. Unfortunately for them, the building was governed by a regulation that required a seven o'clock closing for all offices. At about quarter-to-seven the cleaning man would turn out the main overhead lights and begin sweeping. The knot of heads could be seen gathered in one small office. As they collected around the table talking rapidly in hushed voices under a single bulb, the tableau resembled a somber floating crap game. Then the janitor would whisk them out of there, and they would remorselessly move on to another cubicle. Finally they would be backed up into one tiny cubicle, with every light out but theirs, making their points, until the grim sweeper stood before them and they had to face the fact that the day had ended.

Nearly all of these men had pretty wives, some of them former models, but I didn't know this until a special event took place. It was in the early years of commercial TV, and we were putting on Real Estate's first television show. It was a low-cost half-hour affair, and the idea was to sell houses by television. The occasion had a certain glamour. We watched the technicians moving the cameras around (they wore their caps on backwards, just as in the movies' primitive days). The clock ticked to the hour, the director waved his arms wildly, and we invited guests were conscious of being present at a moment in history.

That the show couldn't have been duller (it didn't sell any houses) made no difference. At the end we were festive. The barbarians' ladies gathered in the lobby. They were fine-boned girls with long white arms, in plumes and black cocktail dresses, chirping excitedly, and everyone was asking: "Where will we go now?" A number of hotel ballrooms and night clubs were suggested.

At this point entered the barbarians, frowning. Their pretty women rushed to them and linked arms. The men looked over the feminine heads and exchanged negative glances. Go where? What's this? Who? Why, nothing like that was planned. Tonight? Impossible. They went off by themselves in their indestructible knot to a hotel ballroom— to hear a speech being delivered by a real-estate operator. The women were put in separate taxicabs and vanished.

I thought of suggesting to one of the disconsolate girls that they get together and pull a Lysistrata on their husbands, deny all love to them unless they agreed to shape up and forget business once in a while. But possibly these men would not notice that anything out of the way was taking place. I have heard enough confessions amid the martinis to guess that great numbers of these obsessed businessmen suffer a loss of sensuality. They appear to undergo a sexual displacement, and no wonder! After all the business and drinking has been done, how much energy do you have to court her?

It is hard for an ordinary family man to compete with a maniac. The nice fellow sooner or later wants to go home; the obsessed one doesn't care if he reaches his front door after midnight. The normal person hopes to live a little; the maniac's drive represents a denial of life. He wants to shut out the simple concerns of humanity, for he lives only in the dream world of his Idea. Also, maniacs tend to have more sheer physical energy than other people, since their efforts are concentrated.

Undoubtedly tyrants have designed the car I drive in, and built the bridge I walk across, and put the buttons on my shirt. Even so, the Crystal Palace is well rid of such slave drivers. The Mediocre Man's Protective League, with all its drawbacks, does permit me to go home to my family and have time to love them.

The lengths to which a tyrant will go to deny life can be fantastic. There was one industrialist who set out to reject and violate the very globe. He requisitioned a transport plane and ordered a contingent of his subordinates to fly with him around the world. No sooner was the aircraft off the ground than he commanded an orgy . . . of drinking. Under fear of his displeasure these executives were in a whirling drunk within a few hours. The carousal continued across the ocean. When the plane touched down in new and exciting lands, the passengers toppled off, exhausted, into hotel rooms where they slept off their enforced dissipation.

There would follow a wobbly inspection of the company's branch office, and whisk, they would be driven groaning to the airport, having seen nothing except from a car window, and off they would soar to another continent; another wild party would get into full swing with the liquor-roaring industrialist urging everybody on. Again, in a third continent they tottered down the ladder like survivors and fell blindly into new hotel rooms, and the process was repeated.

In this way a small tyrant climaxed his career by flying over and insulting the world. He did it in the way they all do, by locking his associates in with him in the cabin of his private world—in this case, finally, a perpetual alcoholic daze.

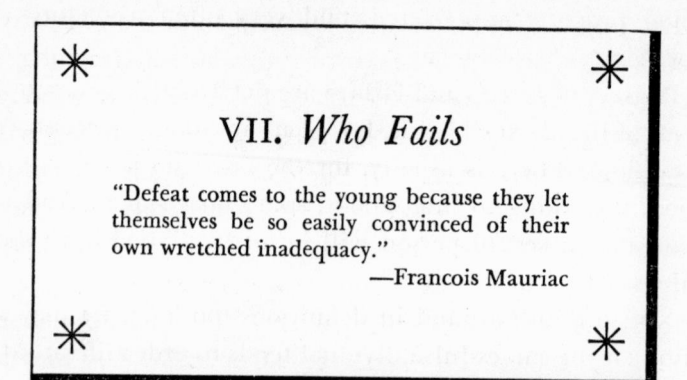

The corporation is kind to failures. It enables them to hold their heads up before their uncles and aunts and the next door neighbors. In a sense our company has abolished abject failure, just as it has done away with glorious success. At the Palace a man who has not risen high may have done considerably less well than others, but outsiders don't know it. In the eyes of the world he is "with the Crystal Palace," which is enough to establish him as a worthy person. Bank clerks are respectful; credit comes easy. Because I belong to the Palace, I am an insider elsewhere. Though I may be an obscure accountant or a submerged baggage-handler in the shipping department, the corporation's prestige shines its light on me. Failure hurts anywhere, but within a corporation it is a good deal easier to take.

Now, unfortunately, comes the time for definition. What is Success and what is Failure? I think they are conditions we can pretty well recognize, even if they are hard to define. This is what I am talking about:

Success involves (a) doing what you want to do and having people respect you for it, and (b) having love.

Failure involves (a) not doing what you want to do, not being properly appreciated, and very often, therefore (b) not being able to love fully.

Degrees of success and failure are determined by combinations of the above. That is, few of us are totally successful or total flops. There is usually, for the one who has not made good, something to brag about, some image-saver. And the generally successful person will in all likelihood have some things to regret.

Not to thrash around in definitions too long, we may say also that the successful individual tends to order life around, while the failure tends to let life order him around. One is usually in command of circumstances; the other usually not. One, who may conceivably have little natural talent, deals with his environment effectively; the other, who may be loaded with talent, can't seem to make it work.

What are the reasons for failure? They are, I think, misplacement and neurosis. The first operates in three ways. A man may be placed in the wrong kind of work; he may have a misplaced image of himself and his abilities; or the authorities—for one reason or another—may have a misplaced image of him.

To repeat, it is a common and frequently helpful experience, particularly at the beginning of one's career, to contend with an ill-fitting job. You stretch and strain and battle, and in the course of knocking about you grow up to become a definite sort of person. It is good to be a well-defined man, as opposed to one of those indistinct carbon copies we find today wandering through the halls of great corporations. On the other hand there can be no pleasure at all in standing revealed as a clearly outlined, luminous failure. But if you venture outside the walls of the Crystal Palace that is the chance you have to take.

Within the Palace you will have small chance of being placed in the wrong job. All the tests, standardized interviews, etc., take care of that. Similarly, the likelihood of your having a misplaced image of yourself is slight. Most corporation people accept without too much grumbling management's appraisal of their value to the company. There will be some bitterness, of course, when one person is promoted over another. I have noticed it especially among the girls who do not seem to disguise their feelings as well as the corporation gentlemen do. When one lady is appointed, say, secretary to a director, her competitors may carve her up for a few days, but like every other strong feeling at the palace, this one dies too after a while.

Nevertheless, inside the corporation and out, the feeling that you are big and *they* treat you small can lead, eventually, to some form of rebellion. The sense of injustice is not necessarily neurotic either, although if prolonged it can become so. Perhaps, indeed, injustice *has* been done. If it has, and the situation appears likely to continue, then the time has arrived to change tactics, or move along to another ranch, or resign yourself to failure.

So far we have been considering sheer incapacity to get ahead, as it has been caused by (1) being stuck in the wrong kind of work, or (2) a wrong estimate of your value, either by you or somebody else. The second major reason for failure, neurosis, is much more serious. The term neurosis, as everyone knows, has been flung in so many directions that it can mean almost anything. It seems popularly to have something to do with "failure to adjust." I am using it in the sense of a self-defeating mechanism in a person.

Without going into the causes of neurotic behavior, I would like to point out that all failures I have ever known in the business world have one characteristic in common.

They languish or drift, sit resignedly, whirl or twist about in a state of *incomplete rebellion*.

The incomplete rebel is someone who resents his situation but can't find the means to improve it. An insurance-claims adjuster, say, would prefer to devote his life to making ship models inside of bottles. But our business culture does not reward makers of toy ships in bottles to any great extent. The rebel has a family and must be "practical." That is, he must do what he does not want to do for the rest of his working life, and this puts him under continuous strain.

Now to pile on another tension. Suppose that a few top fashioners of models-in-bottles *do* make a living out of this obscure craft. Their creations are admired by connoisseurs, and they are held in vast esteem by a small public. Our rebel, we will assume, has an opportunity to study ship-modeling and then perhaps to take the chance of going out on his own and—who knows—joining the select few top artisans in the field. But he hesitates. He can't quite believe that he is good enough. Abysses of humiliation and ridicule open up before him. He feels his children's piteous eyes on him, and sees in his imagination their little mouths open like the beaks of baby robins begging for food that is not there. His wife stands mute (give him this), fearful of his decision. He tries to remember the passage from Emerson's essay on Self-Reliance:

"Society everywhere is in conspiracy against the manhood of every one of its members. Society is a joint-stock company, in which the members agree, for the better securing of his bread to each shareholder, to surrender the liberty and culture of the eater. The virtue in most request is conformity. Self-reliance is its aversion. It loves not realities and creators, but names and customs. Whoso would be a man, must be a nonconformist."

But it is all so unclear and literary. Easy for Emerson, not so easy for us. Besides, things like that only happen in books. With an oath, our rebel flings away his dream. His wife falls into his arms; his children clamber over him, and his friends and relatives smile their congratulations. Then he goes out and settles some more insurance claims.

He does this on Monday, Tuesday, Wednesday, Thursday and Friday, and perhaps Saturday, and then again Monday. . . . By this time the castoff dream begins to poke at him again. He has night fantasies of the ship models he did not make. Every time he passes a cheap model in a store window (he could do so much better with one hand, if they would give him a chance) he looks away with shame in his heart.

Meanwhile back on the job we may imagine that things are not going so well. He begins to dawdle and look out the window. He snaps at an obstinate client. The dreary round seems endless. Perfunctorily going through the day, he arranges a number of inadequate settlements. His boss calls him in for a chat: "Something on your mind? You don't seem to be putting out lately." What can he say—"I want to bottle ship models"? He can't say anything. The warning bucks him up for a while, but inevitably he will drift again. Someone will discover him covertly sketching what appears to be the outline of a Spanish galleon. Sooner or later, with regrets, he will be sent on his way . . . and so he will go circling on and on, himself like a boat caught in an eddy, in the pattern of incomplete rebellion. Some day if he is lucky the dream dies, and the man he might have been dies too.

Is this failure a neurotic? Probably, in the commonly accepted meaning of the term, in that he has "failed to adjust." Yet he would not have been called neurotic during the Renaissance when the skills of an artisan were in greater demand. Unhappily, our incomplete rebel possesses an aptitude and desire for something that has little commercial value. Today, at this time in this place, his natural talents are misfitted, and he becomes a misfit.

He represents a nearly total loss. But there are others who are willing to forget their dreams, and they make a desperate effort to be not-themselves in order to belong. The results can be ludicrous and sad. Such double-dealing of the self may also produce an outcropping of viciousness.

At the advertising agency in earlier days one of our cornerstone accounts was a great corporation noted for its efficiency and stuffiness. All of its male employees dressed in uniformly dark suits and always, I believe by fiat, white shirts. They conducted themselves with an air of sober industriousness, and worked in glass booths so that even the way they sat at their desks could be observed from one end of the office to the other. Signs urging everyone to do his best were hung all over the place, and a terrible atmosphere of decorum hung over everybody.

Once a week the agency representatives met with company executives in a great conference room to discuss advertising matters. These were big meetings, sometimes involving as many as thirty to forty people. A male stenographer, so unobtrusive that he almost managed to shrink into the woodwork, tapped on a silent machine, summarizing everything that was said. The meetings were generally presided over by the company advertising manager, a vulgar fellow, who, like Moon Mullins, always got a laugh by striking a match on Aphrodite's backside. (This seemed to be the one reason for the statue being in the room.) His coarseness was refreshing just the same, amid the hushed personalities of the others.

One day we were talking about a promotion device. The company's choral group had made a recording of the Lord's Prayer. The idea advanced by one of the corporation men was that this recording should be sent as a gift to prospects by the Sales Department. Salesmen would call a few days later, inquire politely whether the Lord's Prayer had been received, and then move in on the prospect, riding a wave of peace and good will.

Our agency group immediately brought up the question of good taste. Sober discussion ensued. At this point up rose an apparition out of the crowd, an astonishing figure of a young man, thin and wild, with crazy hair. He spoke like an evangelist, denouncing anyone who would dare to question the distribution of the Lord's Prayer on any grounds, let alone taste. After all, wasn't that what the Lord's Prayer was for? A company wise enough to associate itself with this eternal message would surely reap benefits. "And well deserve to!" he cried.

It wasn't so much what he said, but his vehemence stunned us. Everyone simply gaped at him, except the stenographer who beat faster and faster on his silent keys. The unbelievable thing was that such a young man could possibly be here, evidently on the company payroll, and could by some miracle be continuing to harangue us, as he did, in one long amazing declaration of principle.

What made it more embarrassing was that his convictions were not at all radical, but on the contrary they were passionately reactionary. He appeared before us as a sensitive apostle of Bad Taste. He hammered on the table to emphasize his agreement with the view of the corporation's nuts-and-bolts assistant sales manager that sales were *everything;*

that, by God, we were all in this business to *make money,* and if the Lord's Prayer helped to accomplish that, so much the better.

He went on. He seemed to want to immolate himself on our altar. I thought of him as a penitent, but most of all as a convert to what he conceived to be the corporate faith. But his breast-beating, of course, only frightened and disgusted the orthodox businessmen. After the advertising manager had made several vain attempts to shut him off, he finally sat down of his own accord with one last thump of his fist on the table. The shattered meeting attempted to pull itself together, but not much more discussion was held on that day. In five minutes proceedings were adjourned without a decision.

Several years later I learned entirely by accident that the fiery young man was living in Greenwich Village. My source didn't have any idea whether he was with a corporation, and knew him only as a struggling poet.

The recognizable forms of incomplete rebellion are virtually without limit and, in varying degrees, they are all forms of failure. At the real-estate office Johnny Macomber gazed out the window for hours on end. He was a mild Texan far from home, and had somehow arrived at this desk with the telephone on it. He was supposed to pick up this phone all day long and call strangers to interest them in buying or selling houses. But he hardly ever called them. He mostly sat and dreamed. Since he was working on straight commission he injured no one but himself, except insofar as he occupied a desk that could have been used by a busier man. Johnny had married a wealthy northern girl, and didn't have to work. But he had to *go* to work, so there he sat, respected by no one. Whenever criticism of his effort arose, he would fix the scolder with the friendliest of smiles.

and turn away to dream some more of the guitars and bunk-houses and the roundups that had once been his life.

Thus, he confronted life-as-it-is with passive resistance. Like Melville's Bartleby, whose identity was smothered in paper work, he finally arrived at the point (although Johnny didn't say it aloud) of responding politely to the demands of commerce with four words: "I prefer not to," and only those words. For all failures in the end would prefer not to; all incomplete rebels prefer not to, but the trouble is that they don't prefer strongly enough *to* do what they would like (if they know). The rebellion does not carry that far.

I remember, also at the real-estate firm, Townsend Blake. His complicated childhood obviously intended him to be an interior decorator. He flounced and preened, and was in fact very much interested in decoration. But he was bound and determined to prove himself in the rugged give-and-take of real estate. Socially he became an *aficionado* of the small fight clubs. He liked to take girls to the fights, and if possible escorted a different girl every week.

In contrast to Johnny Macomber, he was on the phone most of the day but could seldom make a deal. His effeminate manner was against him. Try as he would to disguise his genuine inclinations, they were feminine. Townsend ran from the whole thing. He was all over the place with earthy jokes and slaps on the back; he talked business earnestly. Yet it was clear to anyone, to his colleagues and prospects, that he was putting on an act.

His fakery was worse than ineffective; it became a source of irritation to everyone around him. This is what always happens when the incomplete rebel's image of himself splits off from the image others have of him. There is a sense of fraud. He feels it, and so do the people who meet him. He becomes ludicrous, like a man on skis pointing off in different directions. If he would only go one way or the other, rebel or make peace, or at least make good. But of course he can't. Townsend couldn't. Trying to win the world's approval by being what he was not, he ended up (the last time I saw him) nowhere.

He was soon bounced from the real-estate firm. A few years later I graduated to a small public-relations company. A salesman had been after us for days to switch from manual to electric typewriters. Townsend came in to demonstrate the machine. Formerly plump, he was wan and thinned down. His suit flapped about his frame, and his still-boyish face had on it the same stamp of determination to make good in a way that would be approved by his father. He was still an irritating salesman, although we bought one of the typewriters. He was trying at one and the same time to be Oscar Wilde and George F. Babbitt, both of whom would have laughed at him.

Another misfit in the real-estate company had a strange experience. He was a conscientious liberal, and would have felt at home in a publicity job, say, with the United Auto Workers. But circumstances had pushed him into a company that was the final home of racial and class prejudice. This real-estate outfit was very social and dealt in properties located in class-conscious areas. When the Supreme Court made housing restrictions illegal, a vice-president of the company expressed disagreement with the decision, telling the wire services that "a man has a right to choose his neighbors."

The incomplete rebel who worked under this vice-president found his liberal instincts being affronted every day. He not only had to associate with people who actually believed in discrimination but he also—over his protests that evoked good-natured smiles from the others—had to assist in a minor way in carrying out these policies. But since he had no money and many responsibilities he dared not quit the job.

One day as he sat at his desk a fog fell down on him. It was, he said, exactly like a real fog, and like a wall that separated him from the rest of the world. He did not see others very well, and their activities seemed remote and irrelevant. On top of this was a continuous rushing sound in his ears. He had a floating sensation, "like sinusitis," he explained. It lasted for a month. He went to bed early every night, but that didn't help. He walked miserably through the snow, falling against lamp posts. Even his balance was affected. He tried sedatives; he tried Benzedrine. No good. The doctors told him he was tired.

He went to a psychiatrist, a former army colonel with a cruel, thin mustache and an impatient manner. The young man saw at once that the doctor thought little of him. He had no sympathy at all.

"The trouble with you," said the psychiatrist, "is that you don't want to face life."

"This life!" cried the young man. "Who wants to face it?"

"Precisely, that's your whole attitude in a nutshell. It will be the same in any business, whatever you do."

The doctor was stupid and uncomprehending, and, furthermore, unprofessional in letting his distaste for the patient show so clearly. "This may take years," the psychiatrist said. "I haven't got the time." The liberal walked home disconsolately. He had wasted fifteen dollars on an incompetent father image. It was not until he reached his door that he realized all his symptoms had disappeared.

Within a few weeks he managed to carry on his work so sloppily, in such an anti-social manner, that the real-estate people let him go, and his most immediate problem was solved.

He was right about one thing. The psychiatrist probably did find him unattractive. I know I did. The tensions afflicting incomplete rebels often produce unattractiveness. Frequently their voices become toneless and dead. Failures tend to have stony faces. The heart is cold and suspicious, and its held-in suffering distorts one's voice and manner, walk and dress. With his intimates the incomplete rebel may be lively and charming, but outsiders, those who thwart him, are unlikely to see him that way. He keeps his "real self" at home and "another self" for the office. Day after day he puts on a face to meet the world. Gradually these two separate personalities harden until they become estranged from one another.

At work the failure is estranged from his "home self." At home his "real self" has nothing to do with the painful, frustrating world of business. If by chance his personal and business life come together he may feel panicky. The two worlds must be kept separate or disaster threatens.

A young man I know was agonized by the necessity for inviting his boss to his wedding reception. He felt somehow that his bride would be defiled by the presence of office people. Another could not bear to have his wife visit him in the army for fear that she might see a sergeant ordering him around.

It all has to do with the image of oneself that must not be violated. There follows the assumption that if I have failed some *law* has been violated. Failures are constantly citing Justice, which they believe in but always see not-working. "It isn't what you know, but who you know," etc. The incomplete rebel calls Justice to the bar, and then stands aside to let it argue the case for him, as though Justice were a lawyer with eyes and ears and a commanding voice to prove his case forthwith—instead of using Justice as a club or a stiletto, an inanimate thing to be *wielded* dexterously by him at the right moment. And even then what assurance is there that his justice will prevail in business affairs?

I remember as an inexperienced copywriter being furious because I worked out a campaign, and the account executive who it seemed to me only drank and played golf with the clients took all the credit for it. "Injustice!" I cried out. In a way, yes, but maybe for all I knew the account executive was more valuable than I. There might have been ten dozen copywriters who could have plotted equally effective campaigns, but our account man pleased the client *personally* in a manner that—let's say—could not easily be duplicated. What law could I summon up to prove that my words on paper were more valuable than the account man's charm at the nineteenth hole?

Recently I talked with an incomplete rebel who was in the midst of an extraordinary campaign to prove, through his company's grievance machinery, that his superior had been unfair, and in fact wrong, in his claim that my friend Frank Miller "did not smile properly" in his dealings with the public. The superior had contended on *his* form, filled out in reply to the rebellious complaint, that Miller (a) treated him with contempt (b) had a generally contemptuous manner (c) spoke in a monotonous and hostile voice, and (d) smiled in a way that revealed his disdain for others. Therefore, in the light of these personality defects, the superior wished to downgrade my friend and transfer him to a smaller office where his administrative abilities would continue to be useful, and his grating manner less harmful to the organization.

Miller's contention was that his superior feared his greater ability and knowledge; that his superior was dishonest in certain ways, unsure of himself, and made nervous by the brighter young man who knew he was nothing, which he was. Along these lines he was prepared to fight it out all summer. In a contemptuous and monotonous voice, he explained to me that he was prepared to prove that he did *not* have a contemptuous and monotonous voice. He had Justice on his side. He was going to argue and litigate until the truth came out.

I will back Frank's story anytime. I am sure that his superior is a talentless bureaucrat. Yet curiously enough, as I pointed out to him, there was not much of a discrepancy between the other's story and his own. Obviously the man knew Miller despised him, and this made him nervous. Therefore, he wanted the resentful subordinate out of the way. It was not a matter of justice and law so much as a personality clash. Either Frank had to make up with him, get something on him and crush him, or find another job. But no, he persisted relentlessly: "I'm going to prove. . . ."

Frank refuses to admit that he is living and working in a field of variables. To him, the opposition is a constant, changeless thing. In order to deal with it, he appeals to what he regards as certainties—Justice, Law, Fact, and Performance. He excludes wholly the complicated and volatile relationships between himself and others, as people. He seeks grimly to separate humanity from business. Laws are alive. If he abides by them he should, in all justice, advance.

Frank would find the Crystal Palace a welcome haven. Here a man's value is written down, notated, cross-referenced and reviewed by scores of observers over the years. Their combined opinion bears down on the crankiest of employees with massive authority. Although each opinion tends to be strongly influenced by the one before (and the result can be one extended, massive error), it is still comforting for the rebel to know that everyone is judged in the same fashion, and also that as long as he remains with the company there is *nothing he can do about it.* With no legal action possible, he relaxes. He will suffer no insults and injuries. The company's democratic social organization, which permits him to first-name and expect courtesy from those several ranks higher, helps him to survive disappointments with grace.

Unfortunately, the personality traits of many incomplete rebels give warning signals to personnel specialists at the Palace. Interviewers are very likely to detect stresses and strains in the applicant. If they are not well masked, he will probably be rejected.

The state of incomplete rebellion does not by any means doom us to failure. It may be temporary, or hit us in intermittent attacks in the form of a neurotic fever like malaria that rises and subsides. It may be imposed entirely from without, too. Any healthy man or woman may be paralyzed by indecision, and for a long time. I have known numbers of people who have passed through the experience of "going into the wilderness." They may not pull themselves together for a year or two, or more—that bad period in life from which springs the familiar comeback. How often we hear that someone has, too bad, fallen into a mess . . . and then the news comes in that he has caught hold of an opportunity, and is now doing fine, and we invite him over to the house for dinner.

At the time of my bad period when I didn't have a pair of pants I conceived of an idea that might prove helpful. It was this:

Once a year successful business and professional people, the insiders, should voluntarily undergo a Day of Penance. They ought to don loin cloths and slippers and, along with a herd of goats, shuffle down Main Street in a parade of humility with their heads bowed, giving thanks to the business culture that has recognized their talents. Alongside this parade rebels and failures would run up and down and beat them with bladders. Only on this day, the fantasy went on, would the insiders accept this punishment and it would be a fine release for the community as a whole.

What a bitter and childish idea! When he is distressed, a young man's fancy can take some peculiar flights. But still . . . such an exercise in humility is not unprecedented. Carnivals in which the lower orders run riot and everyone is equal in joy for a day or a week accomplish the same end. The ruling classes of England have used this device for centuries. On Christmas Day officers in a number of regiments serve holiday dinner to the enlisted men. The king and queen and ladies and gentlemen of the court attend the servants' ball. I have seen the rain dance of the Santo Domingo Indians in New Mexico at which village clowns called Koshare submit the elders to various indignities.

Something like that could take place across the length and breadth of America on a certain day—October 31, because Halloween has already become a time of vandalism. (On this evening the teenagers tear down our fences, trample through the garden, and soap our windows. In many communities an effort has been made to persuade the boys and girls to make beautiful soap designs, in a nice way, on designated windows, but this misses the whole point of the October rebellion.)

A Halloween for grownups would be a once-a-year relief from frustration and failure. It might be tied in with fund-raising, and could turn into an exciting, worth while, and therapeutic holiday. For today in America there is no holiday for failures.

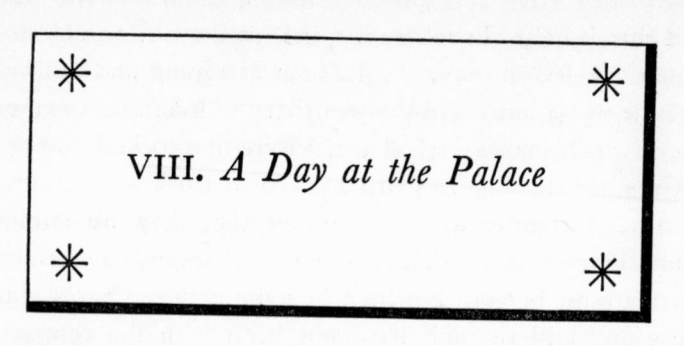

VIII. *A Day at the Palace*

9:00 a.m. The bus-commuters from the railroad station have arrived. Everybody holds the glass doors open for everybody else. We scatter through the great lobby and go down our various beige corridors to the interior and wings of the building. There are two bus-travelers in our department, George Browne and I. The others, like all but fifty or so of the employees at the palace, arrive in their own cars or in car pools.

Our good-mornings are jocular, and if somebody is late we laugh at him. There is a period of settling down. Austin Johnson, the tube-station attendant, grins at us as he arranges his projectiles to start the day. Soon they will be flying through the tube system to all corners of the building carrying pieces of paper, and torpedoes from other offices will arrive at our station with a thump, and a red light will flash on.

The girls are making up and chattering, and it is nice to look at them. Music by Muzak has started up and will give us its soft melodies for the next quarter-hour. Then it will go off for fifteen minutes, and on again, and continue in that fashion until we go home. Thus it is possible to space one's day by quarter-hours. It is said that this music increases office productivity by a sizable percentage, but I haven't noticed that it helps. Probably it quickens the output of those in more or less automatic jobs such as typing and adding-machine work, but I find that if I listen to it at all it puts me in a revery. It makes me feel as if I were in a cocktail lounge.

The girls are slow in getting down to work this Monday morning. I wonder why. It can't be that they are talking about skiing because that season passed several weeks ago. Then it must be golf, bowling, or some dance. They are all pretty and athletic, and have not been with the company long enough to take on the cheerfully resigned look. They have fun and remain irreverent, but must watch out lest they grow too contented with this harmless daily round.

I look out my picture window to watch the late-arriving car pools whirling up the long driveway. The stylish sedans and convertibles hold before my eyes like a snapshot of toy models, cleverly suggesting motion, placed outside the architect's model of our palace to give the "feel" of country office life. The cars will race around the building and find places in the chrome arc of prosperity that half-encircles our office. All our workers have cars, as everyone knows. And our employees also have a view unequaled by any offered to a group of employees since time began. Rolling hills go on to the horizon; they will burst into flower next week, and when autumn comes they will flare red and gold, and winter will put snow on them like frosting. Our landscaped grounds, too, will flower. We can smell honeysuckle; our lawns are so green that they hurt your eyes. Meadows extend to the hills and beyond like a perpetually green future.

It really is time for those girls to quiet down. Walt Comfort who is supposed to be the department's office manager clucks at them but dares not give an order. He will say something like: "Well, I didn't know we were having a three-day holiday." This has no effect. The only way to handle them is to shout: "Hey, quiet down!" in a friendly manner. Walt, a diffident and nice fellow, seldom exercises his full authority. In justice to him I should point out that discipline at the Palace is very lax indeed. People get away with all kinds of laziness and time-wasting without being reproved for it, let alone threatened. For some reason a great many of our executives have no courage when it comes to controlling the loud voices of office boys and inter-departmental loungers.

The chatter is suddenly broken off, and I hear a familiar squeak of shoes. (All our shoes squeak distinctively on the tile floors.) The head of our department, Mac Tyler, is coming down the hall. He stumps past with a gruff good-morning to everyone. The day begins.

I go to my typewriter. In the next office George Browne's machine is already going at top speed. The sound depresses me. George arrived at the Crystal Palace a year ago when he was pushing fifty. He began as a consultant, and has just received permanent status. He found safety here. I like this lively, youthful Teddy Bear of a man whose journalistic career took him all over the world. But then he felt the pressure of time and knocked on the door of the Palace, and now he is sub-editor of our harmless house organ. George says he will leave soon. I hope so. He who has covered invasions and surrenders must work under the aforementioned Walt Comfort who covered lodge meetings for a small-town paper. I must learn to mind my own business, and stop thinking of Justice.

As I start to work, the phone rings. The caller gives me a corrected production figure and I thank him. I will manage to work this into our public-health story. Music by Muzak has gone off and come on again. But it will be some time yet before the coffee cart reaches our area.

Meanwhile I have been unfair to Walt Comfort. He is a good and kind man who has managed small gifts with great skill. His talent is being nice. He is completely a company person, knows the rule book backwards and follows it absolutely. Any violation of the rules pains him, as though he *were* the company. He is, too, in a way. If corporations had an unknown soldier, Walt would be the one laid to rest under our cornerstone. He is unfailingly courteous and never mean to people unless they break a rule, and then only in a mild fashion. If he appropriates credit from his subordinates now and then, the thefts are minor. This petty larceny of credit is done merely to preserve his executive franchise; there is no greed involved. If everyone were like Walt Comfort the world would be a happier place, although there might not be too much going on. I think I have been unfair to him because our department head, Mac Tyler, whom Walt calls "the boss," has recently decreed that I must, among my other duties, help write his house organ. This is a terrible bore.

I am writing a story about the Elbridge family which has been represented in the company for ninety-eight years. Grandfather, father, and son have all been employed by us.

Looking out of the window I glimpse a small event that always makes me feel comfortable. The company limousine approaches the Crystal Palace, carrying the president to work. The black Cadillac rolls slowly to our front door. I can see the president's hand gripping the strap as they turn the corner. The black-liveried chauffeur leaps out and holds the door open. The president alights, followed by the chairman of the board. The president is a serene gentleman with white hair. The chairman has an alert but somber countenance. He makes me think of Scrooge. They stand for a moment surveying the palace façade with complete satisfaction. The president embraces the landscape with one arm, indicating the signs of spring. But the chairman has his eye on something else. He points to the roof. They examine some defect up there with great concern—a leaky gutter. A phone call will be made and action taken, I should imagine, within ninety seconds.

"If Rex Elbridge goes on to normal retirement—twenty-four years hence—the family will have served a total of 122 years. . . ."

This is a bad morning because the coffee cart will not arrive in our part of the building until ten-thirty. We have a half-hour to wait.

10:00 a.m. Coffee! Coffee! Where is that wagon? We all share this preoccupation. When our days extend in an almost unvarying routine I think that many of us develop a minor time-neurosis. We grow accustomed to our routine being partitioned or punctuated in a certain manner. If for some reason the coffee cart does not appear at a certain time, or lunch is delayed, or the Muzak is turned off, or the bus is late, we are disturbed. When routine is violated one's stomach joins in the protest. I find now that I have a perfect craving for coffee commencing at 9:30 A.M. It doesn't matter how many cups I may have had for breakfast; I must still have coffee at that time or I am slightly miserable. The same with lunch. If I cannot go down to the dining room at 12:00 noon I feel a bit dizzy.

Most of us at the Crystal Palace have the same craving for time to stop exactly when it is supposed to. The route of the coffee wagon changes every week, giving departments in different sections of the palace alternate "early" and "late" coffee breaks. This being our late week, I am irritable. Contributing to my mood are the dull chores I must perform in the service of the house organ.

Call this monthly newspaper the *Palace Voice,* since it is the voice of management. Nearly every big company has a paper of some kind, and it is certainly reasonable that such publications should exist. But why must they be so dull? The answer to that is easy: because they mustn't contain the smallest hint of controversy or present any idea that is not pleasing and soothing—"all the news that's print to fit." Every story in the *Voice* has to be checked by higher authority to make sure that it is free of roughage. In the end, therefore, the house organ is like the food in the dining hall— smooth, bland, and creamy.

Well, there can be no scandal in this. Obviously the company is not going to put out any other kind of paper. Management would be silly to question its own policies or crusade against itself. Since the *Voice* deals with the company world and no other, we editors must confine our crusading instincts to denouncing polio and traffic accidents, which we have done without fear or favor. I may also say that we are the poodles of journalism. I was amazed to learn that there is an association of house-organ editors, and that they "confer." About what, I can't imagine. I certainly wouldn't join, for the reason given by Groucho Marx: "I'm not going to pay good money to join a club that lets in people like me."

Coffee! Now I feel better, and a good story has come in. One of our people was in an airplane crash and survived without a blemish. I will interview him in the afternoon. Having joshed with my friends during the coffee break, I return to the *Voice* in a positive frame of mind.

11:00 a.m. Just one more complaint about house-organ editors. After a while they develop corporate reflexes. So does everyone else at the Palace, of course, but it is a shame to see it happen to newspapermen. In his *Inside Russia To-*

day (Harper & Brothers, 1957) John Gunther tells us that Soviet journalists never deviate from the party line because it is also their own line. He points out that:

"The slant comes from within; the censorship is altogether self-imposed. In Moscow, *Pravda* and *Izvestia* have no censor, nor is there any censorship any longer over literary magazines, theatrical productions, and the like, because there is no need for any. The editor of *Pravda* is his own censor, and so is the editor of the magazine. He would not have reached such a post unless his agreement with fundamental state policy was spontaneous, automatic and complete."

Remarkably enough then, the editor of *Pravda* appears to be freer than Walt Comfort and the other editors of the *Palace Voice*. We toe the line too. Even so, we must clear everything with department heads, and if the story is important, with a director. If the editor of *Pravda* can be trusted, why can't we? I can assure you that house-organ editors develop "spontaneous, automatic and complete" acceptance of company policy. We become excellent self-censors. If only given a chance, we could censor ourselves as well as or better than any *Pravda* editor. Well . . . occasionally we slip up, but not often.

For example, one story submitted to a director said that the *Voice* complimented management on a certain move. This was stricken out on the grounds that it implied that the paper had the power *not* to compliment management. Sometimes an inexperienced contributor makes silly attempts to liven things up. Once, writing an account of the annual jamboree I said that a number of annuitants (pensioners) had come around to join in the fun. Among them were John Smith, Bill Jones, Tom Robinson, Old Grand-

Dad, and Old Forester. A feeble joke surely, but our situation breeds juvenile humor. Every authority who saw that line cut it out. Actually, the more I look at the witticism I don't blame them too much. It was their unanimity that was depressing. Another time I wrote that a new span connecting the Palace grounds with the highway would be "our bridge to the outside world." Bam! Again all the blue pencils came down.

I think again without much conviction: "I've got to get out of here!" These rabbit runs of nicety are driving me crazy. I find myself like a schoolboy longing to commit a nuisance. My position is dignified (I ghostwrite speeches for the president to make before great national associations), and I am no longer a kid, but I have to put down impulses to clown and make a fool of myself. This, of course, is immature and, worse, ineffectual. It puts me in a class with that idiot who dropped an open bottle full of ketchup in the tube system, and the other, whoever he may be, who introduced a loose roll of scotch tape into the same wind tunnel.

Everyone asks sooner or later: "Who am I?" I sit at my typewriter and all at once realize that I'm playing the part of a sheer and uninteresting fool, an intellectual playboy. It is a moment of revelation that comes out of nowhere and passes. Nothing appears to change, not even one's expression. Music by Muzak is playing: "We Could Make Believe." But from this hour I know that I will be able to leave the Palace when I want to. Faces are gathered at my door, and my colleagues are grinning at me, which means that it is time for lunch.

12:00 noon. We eat in a gaily decorated dining room on the Terrace (lower ground) Floor, looking out on the side lawn. At one end of the room see our brick-walled Japanese moon gate; at the other, counters for those who wish to eat in a hurry. Most of us go to the assemblage of yellow and gray tables, sit down on bright red or blue chairs, and have a leisurely meal served by waitresses who expect no tips. (Tipping handled by the management.) We look at the menus and fill out our slips, and, still bathed by Muzak, relax.

When we first moved to the Palace a general memorandum (abetted by the *Voice*) encouraged headquarters personnel to mingle in the dining hall and get to know each other. The idea was that you should not necessarily eat with members of your own department, but sit with people doing other kinds of work. This suggestion has largely been ignored. We eat with about the same companions day after day. The result is to pile incestuousness on incestuousness, and our lunch conversations are for the most part, again, as bland and creamy as our food. I do not mean to say that *we* are duller than anybody else, but try lunching with the same group day after day. Conversation becomes a sort of filler, a means of avoiding silence.

Today we are involved in a familiar subject—traffic. Phil Jester was tied up for eight minutes in a jam of cars. Frank Gilliam denounces old men who drive along parkways at twenty-five miles an hour. They are the ones, more than fast drivers, who produce tie-ups and accidents, and moreover you constantly find them driving in the middle of the road. Someone speaks of an accident last week. The amount of time we can spend discussing traffic is fantastic. I think it is because the highway is almost the last place of adventure a suburbanite has left. They are able to talk about their journeys to and from work in the manner of knights, for the dangers are authentic, uncertainties always present, and individual skill is demanded of all.

Also like knights we talk about our chargers. "How is

your old Buick holding up?" Dwight King is asked. Very well, in fact he wouldn't swap it for many of this year's new models. All, all honorable men! Next we go into driveways and lawns and mowing machines and clipping hedges. I am crushed with boredom, for a good reason. Living in the city as I do I don't own any property. Therefore, I can't contribute anything to conversations that deal with virtually nothing else but property of one kind or another. Of course, one is not supposed to discuss Socrates at lunch, but there must be something else. I bring up some plays and movies I have seen—but then my listeners are in the same fix. They practically never go to the movies. It comes down to this: most of the people at our table are good enough to talk with individually, but together at lunch we make the dullest lot you would ever want to avoid.

I notice that dozens of employees at neighboring tables are reading the same pamphlet. It is one of those handouts that are displayed in corporation reading racks. Craning my neck, I see that it is titled: "Are You a Knocker or a Booster?" After lunch I will read it myself.

I forgot to mention that in the beginning it was announced that the gentlemen of the board of directors would eat in the main dining room along with everybody else, although they would have a separate table. On important occasions, such as the need to entertain distinguished guests, they would repair to the Executive Dining Room. This arrangement lasted some thirty days. Now you can't find a director in our eating place. I can understand why, after enjoying one meal in the Executive Dining Room where our department was allowed to entertain newsmen. We had shrimp cocktails and hunks of dripping-rare roast beef compared with the flat chicken à la king featured that day on the menu for lower employees. Rank has its privileges, to be sure, and the first place you can count on over-democracy breaking down is in the food department.

1:00 p.m. In the quiet lounge, surrounded by employees playing cards, checkers, and chess, I will take a long lunch hour and read: "Are You a Knocker or a Booster?" At the far end of this room, shut off by curtains, is the TV annex. Behind me extends the company lending library filled with the latest good books, which I should be reading instead of this pamphlet.

But I am reading in order to make myself angry, and succeeding. As I suspected, "Are You a Knocker or a Booster?" is awful. I don't object so much to the booklet as I do to its distribution. There are a number of outfits that make money by keeping corporations in all parts of the country supplied with this pap. Whoever puts out the tracts must think that the American people are absolute morons. They are so written-down and over-simplified. There would be no reason to mention these booklets except that they are on display in hundreds of racks in corporate halls, and presumably should exert some influence on somebody. Yet it may be possible that they don't. Conceivably not one person has ever been influenced by the messages they carry, and management is being fooled by the pamphlet companies into thinking that their employees find them of more than passing interest.

I was going to detail the plot of this one, but it would take too long. Here is the gist: Mary and Jim are a happy, and you may believe, ordinary young couple. "Mary is proud of her well-paying job with this plant that blends so gracefully with the countryside." Jim (he works too) owns a small service station. They have "three young hellions filled with the exuberance of healthy minds and bodies." The booklet doesn't say who takes care of the children while Dad and Mom are away, not only at work but at all the meetings they attend. For Jim and Mary "never use 'home work' as an excuse to dodge their duties and their obligations to their community and their country."

So much for them. Far more interesting is their friend Ralph, a sorehead. "His take-home pay is larger than ever and he's a likeable guy, yet his friends are worried about a negative attitude that is becoming a part of Ralph." This scoffer is always complaining that " 'the boss is a square,' 'the Mayor's a jerk,' " etc. But he will not join the Town Council or PTA to help correct things.

"His friends are beginning to ask," according to the pamphlet, " 'What's eating the guy?' " They try to explain to him that he ought to become active in community affairs, but "Ralph breaks out with a loud laugh as he says: 'Waste my time, Jimmy boy, listening to a lot of hot air? Not this baby, I got other fish to fry!' "

Where is he off to? Ralph is going fishing. We see Jim pointing to a bulletin-board notice calling attention to the PTA and the Booster's Club. Ralph, with a surly expression, is striding in the other direction with his fishing rod in hand. I can remember when fishing was considered an irreproachably American thing to do, but not in this pamphlet.

Notice, too, that Ralph speaks in a coarse, ungrammatical fashion. I don't think I would like him, and I *do* think it would probably be better for him to be a more active citizen. But I also feel that he has a right to be a slob and a sorehead. We need people like Ralph, if only to point up our own virtues. Following a community get-together, Mary remarks to Jim: "Ralph should have been at this meeting. I think he would have learned why people so strongly resent his negative attitude." (Oh, why not leave the sorehead alone!)

The text rams their point home: "Yes, our behavior pattern can hurt both ourselves and those with whom we have to work and live our daily lives. Are we lapsing into Ralph's objectionable habit of KNOCKING—or are we following in the path of Jim and Mary of BOOSTING?"

Easy to find out. The pamphlet offers "a scientific means," a "Psychological Self-Analysis that we can do ourselves." There follows a test. "Do you sound off about company policies, office politics, your boss' failings—just to impress others?" and so on. All the test questions are loaded in this way. They state an unworthy motive for any sort of criticism. They rule out the possibility that I might sound off on these matters not to impress others but because, for example, my boss actually is a square.

The pamphlets put out by this service also assume at all times that criticism of higher authority is unjustified and neurotic, and even unpatriotic. Thus: "The negative attitude—'it can't be done' or 'the boss is a square'—can be one of the biggest roadblocks to your progress. Worse still, it is contagious and can easily blight your home, your plant and even your community." The crude juxtaposition of these two negative attitudes is typical of the pamphlet's dishonesty. Most knockers complain about the boss either because he seems to them unfair or inefficient. Sometimes "it can't be done" precisely because the boss is a blockhead.

I have taken the test and done much better than I had hoped. The verdict: "You are not a KNOCKER but you veer in that direction. Correct the faults and carefully monitor your tongue. Make a recheck for progress in 30 days."

This has been a long lunch hour. I detect in myself a gold-bricking attitude which I intend to monitor. The reason for goofing off in the army is that the soldier wants to avoid boring or meaningless tasks. This is also true in civilian and corporate life. I never goofed off until I was assigned to the house organ. I am in a dilemma. If I do a good job on the *Voice* I will be stuck with it. Somehow, with this attitude, I have wasted two hours at midday. It is now—

2:00 p.m. A strange and yet ordinary thing has happened. It tells so much about the Crystal Palace. To understand it you have to know something about the character of Phil Jester. I have spoken of many decent men at the Palace. Phil is more than that. This is a man of natural goodness. He does all the right things, not because he has been indoctrinated but because, it almost seems, he was born with a warm heart. We talk about someone's "disposition." Phil is disposed to kindness; he has become a fount of kindness. I have never met anyone with greater moral purity who manages nevertheless a high sense of humor. He is utterly responsive, too, to sadness and tragedy. A former Palace employee died in an oxygen tent without friends or relatives, not a good man, in some ways a bastard, and Phil was the one he called to sit with him through his last day.

With all this going for him, Phil remains a perfect corporation man. Big, heavy, genial, two hundred and twenty pounds, PTA executive, scout leader, officer in the reserves, he is a good father of two, fine husband, excellent drinking companion, splendid one-man audience for you and me, but also, a man who has, finally, not been able to specialize in anything. Instead he has been appointed Mac Tyler's odd-jobs executive in our department. He serves as an occasional shock-absorber (nothing serious) for the boss' bouts of crankiness. Tyler, who standing beside him is as a hydrant next to a tower, looks askance at big fellows and treats Phil with exasperation. But for better or for worse Phil's good heart seems to have neutralized his ego.

Last week he was visited in the office by a charming

woman on an urgent research errand. She was working for a well-known writer who was preparing a book with an industrial background. Our files could supply important answers for her. But Mac Tyler, in a churlish mood that day, had instructed Phil not to give her any of this file material. There was no good reason for his admonition. Nothing she might discover would affect our company adversely. And it happened that Phil had found some of the information she was after.

Today, early this afternoon, it lay on his desk while she talked to him. Plainly her need for the material was urgent. She was warm and attractive, appealing in a mature way, a woman who had been all around the world and known famous people, but who was now up against an assignment that was proving too difficult. With all his manliness he longed to help her. But Mac Tyler had decreed otherwise. He wanted to rise above Tyler's edict, above the system, and respond as a man does to a woman in trouble. He could have killed a dragon for her, he could have (awed witnesses have testified) risen out of his mildness and cleaned up a barroom full of louts, he could have shielded her body with his in any moment of danger, but he *could not* lift his hand and push the file across the desk to her . . . because it was against the rules. He had to watch her go away and accept her thanks for being so good and helpful.

Phil has just come in to me and asked whether he has done the right thing. What can I say? Of course, for him it was the right thing. I want to say to him that I know he has courage. Even so, strong and honorable though he is, only a man with the corporation habit could respond according to the rule book in a situation that cried out for rules to be broken.

3:00 p.m. Once more the coffee wagon, the matched coins

to see who buys, and a meeting called by Mac Tyler. This will be a conference on a company film to celebrate our organization. An outside script writer has been hired to prepare a scenario. I put off my interview with our air-crash survivor, and four of us troop into Mac Tyler's office. The writer waits there nervously. He is a pro with a reputation for turning out solid commercial dialogue, but in hiring him we overlooked one thing. Sick of the movies, he has retreated to the Florida Keys where he has half-built a house. He has returned to do our job only to make enough money in order to complete his project. Hence, his heart is somewhere else and his script outline is nowhere at all. His labored pages tell a familiar story: he doesn't have it anymore, at least so far as our project is concerned.

We trample around in his script for the rest of the day. Soon the writer is out of things altogether and the meeting falls into an old pattern. Jack Reese, the assistant manager of our department, and I versus Mac Tyler; the soft sell against the hard sell. We spend ten minutes trying to prevent Tyler from inserting a line: "Here employees enjoy their good, nourishing food." We maintain that the color close-ups of the food indicate just how good and nourishing it is. The line stays in.

4:40 p.m. Five minutes before quitting time the meeting ends. The bus to the railroad station has pulled up at the front door. There is a mass squeaking of shoes in the corridors. George Browne and I put on our topcoats. Good-by, good-by, good night. On the way down the corridor I ask George what he has been doing. He has been with a photographer topping off a story on an accountant who has had his thirty-year button pinned on him. One of the directors comes down from the top floor to shake hands. The accountant grins and blinks. The flash bulbs go off. Another story, George says, has to do with the company's newest office boy who is looking forward to being the first Crystal Palace employee to retire in the year 2000. I don't know why this story depresses me.

We walk down the front steps toward the bus, and the wheel of the years seems all at once not to turn but to spin before my eyes. Looking about me, I don't have any consciousness of spring but of all the seasons coming upon us faster and faster, and overwhelming us in their quickening cycle. Yesterday the hillside was white with snow drifts, tomorrow it will be green, then parched, the day after for a few moments aflame with glorious red leaves, and then barren and November-hard.

Ten new college boys will be funneled into our hopper, a few pink-cheeked girls will take their places in the typing pool, and out another door will go ten old men and five old women. I may be projecting my own feelings onto them, but it seems to me that the ones stepping into the golden years of retirement have a stunned expression. They smile uncertainly and wave; they put on a brave face, but appear to be struck by the flat blade of time. I have noticed the same expression in milder form on employees who are having decades pinned on them in the form of buttons. It is a vaguely foolish, half-shrewd, half-goofy look, like that of a rube who has had a funny trick played on him at a carnival, and isn't quite sure whether he should enjoy it or not.

We who remain inside can't imagine this sensation. For most of us nothing much will have happened between winter and winter to make this year any different from the last one. At the Crystal Palace we are ignorant of time. We think that we will always have our year, and we are right. All the unnoticed years run together into one unchanging year. Only we age and change. It seems to me now that our group has always been getting into this bus. Oh, we are happy enough. It is just that whatever we do here, we have always done it before.

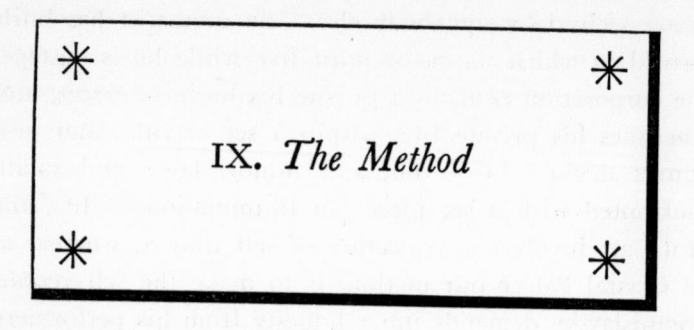

IX. *The Method*

If all the world's a stage, so too the Crystal Palace may be viewed as a corporate theater in which all the actors are bit players. We have no star system here. Even directors and department managers who play relatively significant roles in our endless production never have the stage to themselves. In our show there are always dozens of people taking part in the smallest scene. No one but an insider can tell one actor from another. Yet we have no scene-stealing either. Far from lusting for prominence, our discreet thespians advance by *not* calling unseemly attention to themselves. They play not for the audience and its irrelevant applause but for Stage Management watching from the wings. The equivalent of the stage manager at the Crystal Palace is the Executive Development Committee.

Thus, we have a sort of Method Acting in our company as powerfully and logically conceived as that which has come down to the American stage from Konstantin Stanislavsky and the Moscow Art Theatre. That the two methods are diametrically opposed in their aims and values goes without saying, but their very matching oppositeness, I think, offers grounds for comparison.

The actor and the corporation man have common problems. In the beginning, both are contained within a production conceived by somebody else. The dramatist has built a world in which the actor must live while he is onstage. The corporation man must pursue his business career, and sometimes his private life, within a set of rules and procedures devised by a thousand minds, large and small. Confronted with a set piece, an illumination of life, the actor's art involves a *projection* of self into it, whereas at the Crystal Palace our method is to make the self *recede*.

Stanislavsky demands inner honesty from his performers. The actor must incarnate the role in terms of his own personality. He builds himself into the character rather than merely "playing" the part. In contrast, procedures and protocol at the Crystal Palace teach us to play our parts with inner dishonesty. Just as the actor pours himself into his role, the Palace executive pours himself *out*. He presents to his corporate audience and to Stage Management a walking delegate of the self that he sends to meetings every day. This delegate wears make-up and a disguise. The make-up hides his ego and desire, and in committee smoothly covers his naked opinions. The disguise is that of a team player.

The actor cries out: "Give me Liberty, or give me Death!"

The corporate performer would render the line something like this: "My thought is, I imagine there are some people in our situation who, rightly or wrongly, would rather pass out of the picture altogether, so to speak, than go along with conditions as they are now. Of course, that's only one man's opinion."

Notice in our example (which is not in the least exaggerated) how deftly the speaker removes *himself* from what he is saying. According to Palace standards, he has delivered his lines magnificently, with the lowest minimum of impact. Should a negative reaction develop, our performer can slip back into the crowd scene unidentified with either Liberty or Death. Since other members of the cast have clothed their opinions in similar language, it becomes practically impossible to fix on a hero or a villain. When you have talked with a mouthful of pebbles it is the easiest thing in the world to pretend that you haven't said anything. And, in fact, you haven't.

The Method Actor orients himself to what could be called, I suppose, the "organic reactions" of his colleagues onstage to his own performance. The performer at the Crystal Palace also orients himself to his fellows. But he does not see them as they really are, for they are wearing disguises too. So everybody is relating to a disguised someone else—which is to say that we are hardly relating at all, except in the cooperative advancement of thought. What are we doing? We are, finally, relating to the corporation. *It* is our main audience and our drama teacher; it is The Act that has produced our soporific routine.

Routine is precisely what Stanislavsky wanted to avoid. In *The Evolution of My System,* he explains:

"I am becoming terribly afraid of routine; has it, perhaps, got a firm hold on me already? How can I determine that, if I am not at all certain that I know what this thing called routine is and where it begins, where it springs from, and where to find a way of preventing its deadly roots from fastening in me? . . . Herein lies the problem; to bring life itself on to the stage, but avoid routine (which kills life) while transgressing none of the stage rules."

Here certainly is a problem for all of us, in whatever we do. If we are to embrace life, we must ever be on our guard lest routine's deadly roots take hold. But what can be said for a system that *embraces routine,* and more than that, makes a fetish of it? That is what we do at the Palace, not merely in an administrative way, but in our behavior together, or better say our deportment. In our very hearts we do this. Our hearts come to seek routine. What is Stanislavsky's dedication?—"to bring life itself on to the stage. . . ." In the corporation theater we are dedicated to easing life *off* the stage.

Call this an exaggeration—but are we not all actors in a way, with an image of ourselves, a presence, an individual "act"? When that act goes, what is left for a man, a woman, a girl? Routine. If discontented, one becomes a Frowning Nothing; if content, a Smiling Nothing. One falls into this state gradually. Just as an actor builds himself into his part, so the corporation man if he plays a Nothing long enough will turn into one.

No, when I go to work I must bring myself with me—and the company I work for should give me room and scope to be myself. It is for the company's own good, after all. What do the authorities want with a smiling zombie? Yet apparently, without realizing it, that is the sort of person they do want.

Why? I think it is a result of over-management. At the Crystal Palace The Act has become so big that the actors don't count for much anymore. Perhaps management believes it has a guarantee *in perpetua* of a full house every night, so that it doesn't matter how dull a show they put on. If so, the authorities ought not to be too sure of themselves. The time may come when box office receipts will fall off, and the company will not have the talent and imagination to do anything about it.

Against all this it may be argued that the corporation routine "works." It certainly does, or rather it has, and probably will continue to do so for a while. But I feel that a system that charms the life out of so many of its employees must run into trouble sooner or later for one simple reason —The Act is finally unrealistic.

Corporate practices involve a fundamental inconsistency. Management wants simultaneously (a) performance from everyone and (b) protection for everyone. But the impulse to perform and the impulse to protect yourself cannot exist as equals. One must gain ascendancy over the other. To perform, move, swing, the self goes out and takes chances. The reflex of self-protection produces subservience to the group, a willingness to spread responsibility until it doesn't exist, a binding horror of chance-taking, and obeisance to the system. How can these two drives exist together in equal strength?

The corporation is, therefore, schizophrenic. At Crystal Palace headquarters we drift philosophically between the free-enterprise ideal of the old college try (which we think we have, but we don't) and the aims of a private civil-service state. We think we are staffed with hundreds of red-blooded free-enterprisers. In fact, if we took samples and tapped a few knee caps, it would be found that a large percentage of us have the circulative apparatus of bureaucrats. Instead of blood in our veins we have grapefruit juice. So far as our jobs are concerned, we would be perfectly at home in the most stifling government office in Washington.

Here is an example of our two-headed standard:

One of our notoriously inefficient department heads went on a field trip. He would be away for six weeks. This was a man who made a career out of indecision. Projects piled up on his desk in wobbly towers, and light years went by before he took any action on them. In contrast, his next-in-command was an alert, clean-desk executive who moved quickly on any assignment. A member of the department breathed hopefully: "Now maybe we'll get some things done around here. Norris (the assistant manager) can clear out all those back projects in a week." A more experienced hand smiled at this: "Of course, he could, but he'll never do that. It would make the boss look bad."

A commonplace story, but when you examine it the whole pretense of our structure falls apart. *Theory:* we are all in there pitching for the company, doing the best we know how. *Fact:* the "Method" requires that we *not* do our best because it would make the boss look bad. In other words, the inefficient boss' security is more important than getting the job done. The assistant must subordinate himself to The Act, not do his best, not be himself, for the greater good of the system. It is in this case *ungentlemanly* to serve the company well. And our assistant manager, knowing the game, did hold himself under wraps until his superior returned.

Yet in the face of this sort of thing, the free-enterprise fiction persists. On this faulty ground there has been built, I think, a grand illusion of enormous dimensions. The illusion is that after you have turned people into turnips you can get blood out of them. It is the idea that you can get more out of people by confining them within "proper procedure" than if you loosened the system a bit, gave each employee a personal field of action, and then—at least to some extent—let nature take its course.

What will nature's course be? In our example, with the inefficient department head away on a trip, nature would prompt his assistant to pitch in with a will and clean up the eternal backlog of work. There would be nothing inherently vicious in this act (although it might be undertaken viciously). If it makes the boss look slow, so much the worse for him. He *was* slow. Does the company want its work done or not? We say we do. This assumption is at the heart of our Executive Development program. Getting the job done is supposedly the law governing promotions. But, as Mr. Bumble said, "If the law supposes that, the law is a ass." The truth, as I have seen it work out in practice, is that in a crisis most of us are far more loyal to our pension programs than we are to doing a job in what we believe to be the best way. Naturally we prefer to do the best thing, but we prefer even more not to rock the boat. Sometimes for us the most rewarding decision is no decision—anything to avoid the lonely prominence of commitment.

The grand misconception here, I think, must be the one that says: "Organization is all." This has led to all the propaganda on the virtues of team play. We must have teams, yes, but I am always suspicious of the halfback who scores three touchdowns on long runs and then sobs in the dressing room: "What do I care? The team lost!" I think he is pretending, and will go home quite pleased with himself. Following, too, from the team play concept is the corporate emphasis on experience. It will be said of some dunderhead that he has been seasoned for twenty years in his department. This is like a football coach with a rotten team last year looking forward with confidence to the fall campaign because he has "twenty lettermen returning." That impresses me not at all. Preserve us from such lettermen. If they were no good last year, particularly in the upper age brackets, they will be worse this year. No, I think any organization must make room for stars, lots of them, make way for the old ego, otherwise we will have to face up to the space age with a bunch of turnips on our payroll.

But in our way at the Palace we spend great sums of money to build a good team. We go about this via the Executive Development program. From time to time guidebooks are circulated. Would you like to know how you are developed? The following paragraphs are based on a typical "Executive Development Guide."

The Guide begins with a set of unchallengeable assumptions:

> "The creation and perpetuation of a high-caliber management team cannot be left to chance. It calls for a well-planned, well-accepted, positive program of executive development. . . . It calls for frequent realistic appraisal of each individual performance and potential. It calls for bold development action incorporating demanding, capacity-stretching assignments coupled with sound counseling. It calls for discerning use of rewards. . . .

> "Continued prosperity can only come through the efforts of a management team of highest caliber; through men with imaginative, shrewd analytical minds; through men who are interested in hard work, profits, and keeping ahead of competition. . . ."

So far, so good. There is no question that the development of high-caliber management "calls for" these various qualities. But who is doing the calling and who is doing the answering? Management is calling and management is answering. In short, management is talking to itself. Again, so far, no harm done.

The progress and the *predicted development* of each employee are appraised at regular intervals by his boss, his immediate supervisor, and perhaps "a third person on the level of the individual's supervisor who is well-acquainted with the individual's performance." At first glance this would appear to be a fair arrangement. It theoretically provides for three separate and independent reports on a man. If, say, his boss doesn't think too much of him, his supervisor and the third party may redress the balance with favorable appraisals. But this in practice will seldom happen. We may as well say it can't happen, because:

> "It is recommended that each member of the appraisal panel first prepare his appraisal by himself and then meet with the other panel members in formulating *the joint appraisal.*"

Clearly the last provision negates all that has gone before. It serves also as a good example of the corporation's extraordinary capacity for deceiving itself. To show how the system works out we need only imagine a scene with four characters: Allen, the department head; Barclay, one of the department supervisors, and Clifton, the third party, also a supervisor. All three are meeting to draft a joint appraisal of Danforth, a junior executive.

Allen, the boss, either low-rates or overrates the young man. Barclay and Clifton, who observe his daily performance, disagree. Their private appraisals of Danforth vary markedly from the department head's view. Now enters a new factor. Allen is *also* going to fill out appraisal forms on his two supervisors, and they know this. Can you imagine them disagreeing with the boss at length on the Danforth appraisal? With the appraisal of their *own* progress coming up? No, the chances are infinity-to-one that, with their training in corporation method-acting, they will gracefully withdraw or modify their evaluations of Danforth (without seeming to do so). It is more than likely that the joint appraisal will turn out to be pretty much in accord with the boss' judgment. Pursuing this, we may wonder how he measures his subordinates.

"One of the most distinguishing characteristics of the outstanding manager is his constant appraisal of employees. . . . Members of management are judged by their superiors, in large part, by their ability to set high standards, to appraise others accurately against such standards, and to take constructive action to build a strong team."

We are graded in this way:

Performance Ratings	*Potential Ratings*
A—Outstanding (*rarely equaled*)	A—Outstanding
B—Well above average	B—Considerable
C—Satisfactory	C—Some
D—Unsatisfactory	D—Limited
?—Undetermined	

We are judged according to our Intelligence, Motivation, Relationships, Administration, and Knowledge. There follows a graph showing that Intelligence is about 90 per cent innate and 10 per cent acquirable; Motivation 80-20; Relationships 65-35; Administration 35-65, and Knowledge 10-90. Bearing this in mind, the company must employ "only those applicants possessing superior intelligence, exhibiting extraordinary motivation, and indicating promise in the area of relationships."

Now this is a fine graph, and the conclusion drawn from it appears unassailable. But what has all this to do with reality? The plain fact is, and you gentlemen on executive-development committees must know it, that the corporation employs scores of individuals with mediocre intelligences, the motivations of squirrels, and the relating powers of amiable zombies.

My main objection to the Executive Development program is that is does not visualize people *as they really are*. It assumes that people are neutral spirits and ignores the strongest motivating force in our private civil-service state, which is self-preservation. Years of method acting at the Palace may teach us to avoid being ourselves, but they also tell the walking delegate of the self to keep his place in line.

For this reason we model ourselves in the image of our superiors, as we follow in their footsteps, and expect subordinates to model themselves on us. This much is human nature: an executive is going to file a good report on an underling who thinks and acts more or less in the way he does. And he will tend to give a lesser rating to someone who thinks and acts differently. Executive Development planners, who are not stupid, have been aware of this, and we have seen how they try to counterbalance it by the system of triangulation. But, unfortunately, no sooner do they triangulate on a man than they abandon the principle, for the verdict must be unanimous. The Act at the Crystal Palace does not permit a single crack of executive disagreement to be revealed to the audience; no minority opinion (there probably wouldn't be one anyway, after the joint-appraisal session ended) may be filed. Appraisers may differ, yes, but:

". . . any large variation can only result from an inadequate understanding of the appraisal factors and system or the appraisee. (!) Variations can be minimized by developing among appraisers a uniform understanding (?) of the appraisal system and by omitting ratings for those factors about which the appraiser has insufficient knowledge of the appraisee."

Translated, the last sentence means: "You fellows get together on this. If you disagree, one or two of you can avoid an embarrassing situation by taking the 'out' provided here —namely that you don't know enough about the young man to rate him in certain categories."

Once upon a time Free Enterprise invoked the principle of the Survival of the Fittest. Today at the company we have the survival (or rather the promotion) of the Most Imitative. The question before the Executive Development Committee when promotion time comes is how snugly you will fill the shoes of the man above you.

"The individual is compared with all known executives in the next higher level of management and the appraiser should form a judgment as to how the individual would stand in such company.

"Reduced to simple terms, the above implies that an individual with a superior performance rating in his present position . . . will very likely produce superior performance in a more demanding assignment. At the same time, the above warns against being overoptimistic as regards an individual who exhibits a high rating in intelligence or knowledge but does not have the support of a good performance record, or an individual who is performing very well in his present position but does not have the desired mental or other resources."

See how reasonable our promotion system appears on paper. Therein, I think, lies its major fault. For it is people, not animated sprockets, who must carry out these admirable procedures. The system assumes, I can only say naïvely, that each executive will appraise others in an entirely disinterested manner, keeping in mind the company's interests, not his own. Palace in Wonderland! Executives simply don't act that way. Nobody acts that way. The most cooperative men and women in the world will, in their own small fashions, look out for themselves first and the company second.

In surveying his team almost any executive is going to appraise it so that the men below who might challenge or deviate from his method of doing things will be put in their proper places. His instinct, if not his conscious aim, will be to favor those below him who appear to be smaller replicas of himself. A final quotation from our Guide:

> "In the process of being concerned about standards, past performance, and the resulting impact that one's appraisal has on the destinies of one's subordinates, the appraiser is caused to think more carefully about his own work, his goals, and his own needs for self-improvement. A highly penetrating appraisal in itself thus tends to bring about improved performance on the part of the appraiser. . . ."

So far as I have been able to observe, nine times out of ten the appraiser "is caused" to do no such thing. He is caused mainly to arrange his appraisals in such a way that his superiors will think he is doing a good job. But even suppose that he is prone to self-criticism and confessions of inadequacy, in the manner of a Soviet official who has failed to meet his quota—will this necessarily improve his appraisals of others?

The old question is, can thought understand the nature of thought? Similarly, can a corporation man properly appraise a subordinate more intelligent than he is? If not, what can the subordinate do, particularly in the early stages of his career, to get around these inadequate appraisals which affect not only his present status but also to an important degree his future? Answer: he can do nothing. He is like a man on a slow escalator with someone in front of him who will not move.

In a smaller and livelier business the held-down subordinate has better possibilities of extricating himself. The free play of personality is greater; he has a chance, positively, to run with the ball and call attention to himself, and negatively, to cut, backbite, and take a chance on showing up his superior. But at the Palace the uses of power are restricted to channels, much like the army. There is one small difference. The army, recognizing this situation, has an Inspector General's office. Officers from the IG may visit installations and—since they are independent of the base command —listen to criticisms and complaints. True, they may seldom take action, but still the IG office exists, just as the chaplain exists, and if their roles are often viewed derisively by the rank and file, they serve as something of a deterrent, at least theoretically, to inefficiency and injustice.

Perhaps corporations might do well to institute some sort of IG system, an outside audit not only of the books but also of administrative performance. What is needed, I think, is a means of periodically going outside the chain of command to evaluate efficiency up and down the line. At the Palace, annual reports of plans, achievements and profits are, of course, furnished stockholders. But these annual reports, with irreproachable intentions and the greatest efforts toward honesty, must still be dressed up in their Sunday best, and they may not reflect the administrative picture at all. This does not indicate laxity or slipshod reporting on the part of top management. In fact, supposing that anything is wrong, the men at the top may be wholly unaware of deficiencies in the lower echelons.

In an article, "The Jungle of Hugeness" (*Saturday Review*, March 1, 1958), Dr. Kenneth E. Boulding, professor of economics at the University of Michigan, has said that one of the major weaknesses of large-scale organizations likely to manifest itself in heavy weather is the breakdown of the internal communications system. He points out:

"One of the main functions of organization is to *prevent* information from reaching the executive; all the way up the hierarchy information is lost by condensation and abstraction although, supposedly, relevant knowledge is returned. In the process, however, there are abundant opportunities for distortion."

Why are the facts often distorted?

"This happens not only because of the natural frailties and incapacities of the human organism as an information and knowledge transmitter but also because of the *dependency* of the lower ranks of the hierarchy on the higher. A 'boss' depends for his proper functioning on information supplied to him by the 'bossed,' and yet the bossed depend on the boss for their jobs, their possible promotion, and possibly their livelihood. It is not surprising, therefore, that the boss often receives the information that his subordinates think will please him, rather than what they think is true."

Misinformation may be conveyed from middle- to top-management in many ways and for all sorts of reasons. I recall an able but vain and impatient executive who was involved in installing a company's new filing system. The files were his pride and joy, and beautiful interlocking numbers floated through his dreams. The company was also starting a library, and hired an expensive and fiercely proud librarian. The executive and the librarian who worked under him collided head on. The issue was whether company reference

books should be classified in accordance with the newly installed filing system or whether they should be arranged in
the time-honored decimal groupings used by libraries everywhere. After a protracted struggle, the librarian won, but
made an enemy. Thereafter, in commenting on the librarian's work, the executive passed upward the general image of
an uncooperative, neurotic, temperamental dragon. These
images of the librarian were clothed in the discreet language
of our Method (damnings with faint praise, etc.), but the
truth as conveyed upward was influenced by thwarted ambition, and there was no way for the librarian to re-draw the
picture for the gods to see.

Feed questions into a neurotic Univac and you would receive neurotic answers. Our managers and appraisers are
not even Univacs, but are nevertheless expected to function
like unemotional calculators of what is best for the company. The Lord knows they try, and we all try to conduct
our business with moderate and retractive personalities,
with masked egos and (most of us) orderly ambitions. But
behind our discreet performances you may be sure that we
are always conscious of the stage manager. The reflexes of
self-preservation will guide our movements and flatten our
dialogue, and shape our opinions and reports, and it is
foolish to think that they will not.

It will always be so until such time as a Stanislavsky from
the Mt. McKinley Business School issues a call for all of us
at the Crystal Palace to build ourselves, organically or any
other way, back into our roles of driving, slightly fearful,
egoistic individuals trying to get ahead of one another; until
we are no longer every one of us bit players; until we abandon this "stab, grab, and apologize" Method of ours.

I think what the Crystal Palace could use right now would
be a court jester, a wild card, to upset the order of our

days. We could employ a Catskills *tumler,* a camp joker, a friend-of-presidents type, even a fool, whose job would be to bring irreverence to our halls. He should be permitted to make fun of everybody, great and small, to mock every process (in an irresponsible way), to call a spade a spade, dramatize errors, to stick his head in conference rooms, interrupt procedures with a wisecrack and vanish again. You would never know when he was coming. You might not see him for weeks or a month in your department, but you would know that he was somewhere in the building. The corporation joker would be an irritant to our complacency. Cutting capers across our routine, he wouldn't really disrupt the system. Yet he would shake it up a bit.

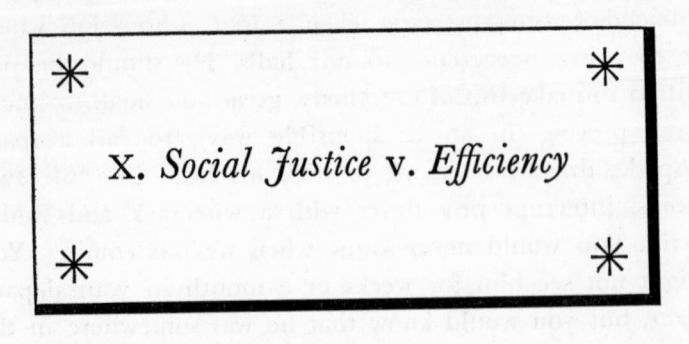

X. *Social Justice* v. *Efficiency*

What are you going to do with a fifty-year-old man who doesn't have it anymore? Throw him out of the operating group or retain him? If he is retained, in what capacity should he serve?

This is a problem that has confronted organized man since his bearskin days. It has also concerned organized beasts. The old bull or walrus dominates the herd until a strong youngster topples him, whereupon the vanquished one limps away to the edge of the organization and subsists as best he can. Thus, in the animal kingdom performance is all. The animal puts out until he can't anymore, and then he's had it.

Rising from the animals, we know the tribes that are said to put the decrepit grandfather on an ice floe with a bar of chocolate. Others have left the old and unproductive by the side of a trail with a blanket to cover their final misery. Again, performance is everything. We have a name for these practices; they are barbaric. If we judge tribes, including our own, by the way they care for their unproductive members, those who temper performance with mercy may be called civilized, and those who judge by performance alone purely barbaric.

There are, of course, extreme situations like the familiar one of the lifeboat adrift in a stormy ocean in which (a) incompetents may be thrown overboard to save the rest, or (b) incompetents (classically, in this milieu, women and children) are saved, and strong men gallantly cast into the depths by the crew, or (c) everybody draws lots, in which case, by luck, crones and graybeards may survive and great artists and beautiful women be tossed to the sharks. It is hard to say whether the selection of those to be sacrificed is civilized or barbaric, but at any rate the emergency is real and, barring a spiritual decision that all should die together in the overloaded boat, can't be solved in any other way. You have to form a committee, devise a system, and choose. That's civilization, so far as I know.

In our time we have become profoundly concerned with insuring Social Justice for everyone. Nowhere will you find a stronger sense of social justice than at the Crystal Palace. In our time, too, we have become not merely concerned but obsessed with techniques of Efficiency. And nowhere will you encounter a greater preoccupation with efficiency than at the Crystal Palace.

But the ideals of efficiency and social justice are frequently in direct opposition. Social justice involves recognition of a person's right to survive even though he may not be productive, while efficiency demands that we get the job done in the best way, justice or no.

In the corporation we assume that an employee has put in years of conscientious work, and that, therefore, if he has slipped to the point of uselessness we must still recognize his earlier contributions. We ought not to throw him out, nor should management insult or injure his pride by reducing his status, unless a clear emergency arises. This humanitarian policy considers the dignity of the veteran himself and, besides, reminds younger employees that they will be treated in decent fashion until the day they retire.

In the corporation we also assume that our business will be conducted with the greatest possible facility. Endless paper work, memorandums and reports of all kinds are directed toward that end. If necessary, we will detail ten employees to see that twenty others do their jobs well. Yet although we are devoted to doing a good job, we believe no less devoutly that it need not be done at the expense of our employees' welfare and dignity.

At the Crystal Palace, then, one of our basic principles is that efficiency and social justice are compatible. Here we sometimes run into trouble, for situations do arise in which quick executive action is called for, and the beneficiaries of social justice *cannot respond*. When this happens, in one way or another the company loses money. We now discover an interesting and heartening phenomenon. The corporation is apparently willing (without admitting it) to lose a certain amount of money in the interests of preserving social justice. The record shows that we will be satisfied with something less than maximum performance in order to treat our employees in a humane way. In short, we settle for optimum rather than maximum performance. Could any organization in history offer a finer epitaph?

The optimum is the best possible—a condition that changes from day to day. The best possible performance (consistent with humanitarian principles) of a company may be very different today from what it will be five years from now. Our job at the Crystal Palace, after all, is to make money. So long as the corporation maintains a high rate of earnings it is "possible" to subtract humanity-money and still come out well in the black. But if, over an extended period, earnings drop it will no longer be feasible to lose money out of kindness.

When earnings fall, optimum and maximum performance merge; they become the same. Nothing less than the maximum will do if the company is to survive. On that Day of Judgment, as surely as an apple drops off a tree, funds for humanity will be cut down and a certain number of human beings will be cut down too.

To avoid this, management must remain as alert, healthy, and strong "as possible." That is, it can afford to carry only a certain number of inefficient employees on the payroll. If the organization accumulates too much lead in its bottom it won't be able to move fast enough. If it assembles too many layers of fat in its head it won't be able to think quickly. In this state it qualifies for possible extinction. No matter how generous their pension plans may be, employees of a thick-headed, fat-bottomed corporation are living in a fool's paradise.

At the Crystal Palace management's built-in humanity is above reproach. A good question, however, is whether we are approaching the danger point of overloading our ranks with mediocre personnel. If so, our structure will someday begin to lean. Numbers of us will be sent packing with our savings tied in a red handkerchief to face a competitive world we have not known for years.

But that day, let's hope, is still a long way off. It need not come at all if management stays in shape. This may be done by maintaining not exactly a lean and hungry body but an organization not too fat with kindness and complacency.

Why does an executive become inept? I have seen these causes at work:

1. *He never was any good.* This one often has connections.

He may be somebody's nephew or golfing companion. A product of easy-going times, he's generally amiable, gives his subordinates room to move, leans on their judgment. Postpones decisions, and when confronted by matters not covered explicitly in the book may become paralyzed. Despite his good nature, is disinclined to back up members of his staff in an interdepartmental showdown. Normally easy to work for, but unless he has forceful assistants not much work will be done in his office. Discipline bad.

2. *The job is too big for him.* He's in over his head and knows it. Spends much of his time trying to disguise his ignorance of what is going on, but fools nobody. May act in a capricious manner, flying in the face of reason to assert his authority. He may also exhibit paranoiac symptoms—suspicion that others are trying to get around him (which is often true) or show him up. In many instances he has a fluctuating list of favorites, but none can stay close very long lest they discover his lack of confidence. His decision-making is unpredictable, for he may be too slow or too quick. Tends to get out on a limb and hang there stubbornly. At these times he can't move, won't think. Discipline good, morale uncertain. On occasion salves hurt feelings by some generous act like granting unexpected credit or time off, or throwing a staff party.

3. *Years of routine stupefy him.* This executive has reached a plateau and probably will remain there. He knows exactly what his job is all about, or rather what it has been in the past, but will not respond to changing times. Believes in doing things just the way they have always been done. Cannot abide new methods unless they are countenanced by the book; even then may resent them and drag his feet. Slow thinker. Handicapped by sheer lack of imagination. Has all but forgotten the profit motive which

has been swallowed up in his mind by the niceties of administration. Departmental discipline automatic. Output steady but slow. Office morale dull but not in pain.

4. *He is corrupted by complacency.* A cut above the routine executive, he is the Narcissus of the Crystal Palace. He admires his image to such an extent that he cannot bear to have the least scratch on his record. Consequently, will not act unless sure that the move will put him in a good light. Utterly satisfied, primps before the mirror of his past performances. Frederick the Great said the trouble with war is that it spoils armies. Similarly, for this handsome man the threat of decisions lies in their possibly disarranging his appraisal form. Intelligent and ambitious. Eyes board of directors; hopes to reach that status by means of imposing administrative good looks. Formal with subordinates, he keeps them in their place. He is inhibited by selfishness and conceit. Office discipline good. The staff is often intimidated.

5. *If progress is recognized, life has no meaning for him.* He held a key post in the past and made his mark, but time has reduced the importance of his specialty. He cannot accept this. Retains loyalty to outmoded techniques that made him important. Despises new methods that tend to diminish him. Will not compromise, and frequently becomes rude and uncooperative. Surpassed by smoother, younger men, senses their relative lack of originality and lets them know it. Crusty, he may have the affection of a few older employees. A source of embarrassment. Departmental discipline poor. Morale not good. A chauvinist and a throwback to primitive capitalism, he is the most likely of all inefficient executives to be retired early. Admirable, impossible.

6. *He is aging and losing his powers.* Not sick enough to be retired, his senses have grown dim. His thoughts repeat

themselves, falter, and go off in irrelevant directions, particularly near the end of the day. Fears younger men, but they nevertheless handle him with ease. Occasional revivals of strength confuse the issue—that he is no longer as intelligent as he used to be. Can be gotten around, although he may offer unexpected resistance. Office discipline poor. Morale middling to poor. Departmental output not good enough.

All of these executives in varying ways become administrative road blocks. Should a number of them block at the same time the organization suffers a localized thrombosis which may cost a great deal of money. More likely, their inefficiency produces a series of little strokes which may not greatly impair the company's operations at the moment, but weaken it in the long run.

In times of emergency, however, these Road Blocks can cost us our very lives. Going outside the Crystal Palace, I remember the first atomic bomb test at Bikini in 1946. I was one of many reporters to be amazed by the following inincident.

The U. S. Navy was running the test and had assembled a flotilla of target vessels spaced across Bikini Lagoon and out to sea. The Air Force dropped what is now considered a very small atomic bomb which burst in the air over this fleet. Relatively few ships were sunk, *no* battleships, although awesome damage was inflicted and the radiation count near the target center was hellish. But looking at the results through binoculars on the first day, observers didn't have the impression that they were extraordinary. A high-ranking Navy officer strode into the wardroom of the press ship and declared with an air of satisfaction that can only be described as fatuous: "Well, I guess that shows that atomic bombs can't sink a fleet at anchor." An Air Force officer who heard this sprang at him, and they had to be separated.

Now, supposing the Navy man to be intelligent (he *had* risen to a conspicuous rank), this shows how far road-block thinking can lead good men astray. It turned out that he was a partisan of the battleship. Not a stupid individual under normal conditions (nor were those who court-martialed Billy Mitchell naturally stupid), he simply could not bear to believe that this new-fangled atomic-energy business could destroy what he had labored to build. A good man, let's say he was. The meaning of his life was more important to him than survival. Such a man deliberately misinterprets the evidence of his senses.

A similar road-block story was told to me by a doctor. It had to do with an eminent specialist, a connoisseur of a dangerous disease. He had built his career around this disease, and had come to love it as one loves a necessary enemy. He knew its most intimate moments, its temperament and willful tricks. He could measure the honor and significance of his life in terms of the grateful patients he had saved from the disease he loved.

One day the younger doctors came to him with news of antibiotics that when used experimentally had brought about dramatic overnight victories over the enemy. The specialist smiled indulgently. "Gentlemen," he said, "I have seen these so-called cures. They come and go. . . ." But the young men respectfully insisted. The antibiotics invariably had an astounding effect, and smothered the disease as though it were nothing. The great doctor scoffed: "Go ahead. You have my permission to use this new what-you-call-it. You'll find out. . . ."

They found out that the new drugs virtually abolished the beloved enemy. No more subtle analysis was necessary; no delicate intuition was required. All you had to do was fire in the miraculous injection. The doctor stood aside, thunderstruck at the swiftness with which all his lore and learning had been swept into retirement. Not long after that, for whatever reason, he killed himself.

He was a magnificent Road Block. His counterparts at the Crystal Palace have no such grandeur. He was a big man; they are relatively little men. He was protecting his science and his art of healing; they are protecting only their functions.

Seeing the Road Block in action at the palace, you find it hard to feel sorry for him, because the company's benevolence secures him against suffering. He will not have to pay the consequences of his ineptness. Recently the company undertook a major project. The ultimate cost of doing the job exceeded carefully worked out estimates by over *seven million dollars*. The Crystal Palace is a wealthy organization, but not so rich that an unscheduled laying out of that amount doesn't produce an extremely painful dent in the books. It would seem that somebody must have been negligent or incompetent somewhere along the line. Either those who made the estimates were unrealistic, or not properly informed, or those who carried out the project were woefully lacking in some way.

We may concede that a number of unforeseen outside influences pushed up the cost of the undertaking. Even so, our planners are paid to anticipate and make allowances for at least some of these developments. Yet the gentleman in immediate charge of the job did not suffer any loss of prestige. There never was so much as a rumor that anyone was held personally responsible. Here, once again, we come upon the corporation's device of spreading responsibility. And, in truth, it probably *would* be unfair to make any one individual the goat for the organization's failure.

Yet without knowing the inside story I am quite sure that

a sizable portion of the blame could be assigned to our loyal, semi-anonymous team of Road Blocks. These veteran lettermen—each in his own small way—were in a position to contribute to the fiasco. By refusing to make decisions, not hustling, not thinking, or otherwise failing to do their jobs properly they helped waste enough money to pay their pensions from now until doomsday.

I think we are entitled to insist that walking, breathing human beings and not merely "circumstances" had something to do with our vanishing seven million. We may also insist that there can be no excuse for miscalculations involving a gigantic outlay of that sort. One is tempted to say (but must not, I suppose): "To hell with social justice— let's move a few of these blockheads *out of there*. We want a winning team!"

Easy to say, but how are they to be moved out? Under present conditions at the Palace, you would actually, physically have to dynamite our Road Blocks out of their positions. Even then, with the adhesive power they have, you couldn't be sure of blasting them loose. The trouble is, you would be requiring the organization to put dynamite under itself, and that is too much to ask.

Our problem then is how to call a halt to incompetence without injuring anyone. One of the finest men I know recently suffered through this dilemma. Some years ago he took on a position in a California appliance firm that was being extensively reorganized. He was informed by the board of directors that he could make any changes he wanted, but in order to hire new men he would have to fire an equal number of veterans. He found that his labor force was made up of a crew that had been intimidated for fifteen years by his predecessor. Key men had been frightened out of the talent they had originally possessed, and seemed incapable of doing anything on their own. They virtually raised their hands for permission to go out to lunch. Worse, their performances were timid and lackluster and the new plant supervisor had to work far into the night and revise his schedules. He was and is a clear-thinking and forceful executive. His difficulty is that he can't stand the idea of inflicting pain on anyone. Time and again he made up his mind that he would have to unload some of his less talented technicians. But when he saw how nervous they were and calculated that by firing them he would cost each one an average of fifty thousand dollars in savings of one sort or another, he couldn't go through with it. As it turned out, the warmth of his confidence saved the day. With the thawing of fear, his assistants experienced a revival of their frozen abilities. This was a time when compassion paid off.

Has there ever been a society that has perished from too much mercy? I think the Crystal Palace is running that risk. To help ward it off, we must find a way to get around Road Blocks without violating their rights. But what are their rights? It seems to me that we should distinguish between a man's (a) vanity (b) honor, and (c) subsistence. Assume that he has honorably served the corporation for fifteen or twenty years. In the interests of company performance, I think we may be allowed to impair his vanity but not his honor, and we certainly must not, according to our lights, threaten his livelihood. In short, we may not knock him down but we can move him sideways.

The difficulty is that it becomes expensive to move Road Blocks sideways. Appoint them to special commissions, send them on inspection trips, and you are still wasting money. It might be better to establish a system of dual administration, one charged with action, the other with maintenance. Move the Road Blocks over to the Administrative Maintenance side. The system would envisage the counterparts of a prime minister and president for each department. Give the president the title, and give him a larger salary than the prime minister. (The Road Block, who is usually older, already has a higher salary anyway.) The Road Block would serve as an elder statesman, with control over the administrative apparatus. He would be the department manager, chat with distinguished guests, greet visiting boy scouts, etc. He would also have the power to recommend and comment on the action initiated and carried out by the assistant manager and his group, but he would have no power *over* the action. That would not be his job. If things didn't pan out as he had predicted, he would be entitled to say: "I told you so," and file a report. But his most important contribution would be to *stay out of the way* of the action group.

In this manner a road-blocking executive could be kicked sideways, retain his honor, and at the same time be able to do worthwhile work busying himself with administrative matters. This would be no hardship. After a certain point in time most of the road-blockers come to enjoy housekeeping duties. In his turn the younger action-man would be free of administrative details, would not have to greet boy scouts, and could move ahead on his job with a minimum of interference.

If the Road Block's vanity suffered, that would be too bad. Our reference points are justice, human dignity, and efficiency. He has no right to the name of action who spends his days inhibiting it.

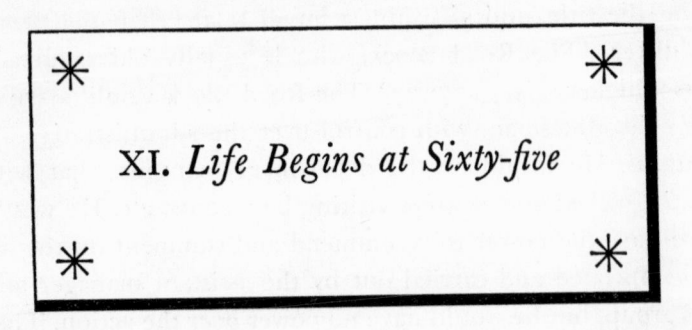

XI. *Life Begins at Sixty-five*

One day several of us were conferring with the boss, Mac Tyler, in his office on the proper organization of a guided tour through the Crystal Palace when a strange face appeared in the doorway. It was a mournful face, brown and drawn with age. The man on the threshold squinted at us and took a few steps into the room. Uncertainly he said: "Hi there, Mac."

Mac Tyler looked up impatiently from his diagram of the corridors. His expression changed instantly as he recognized the visitor. "Art Blackburn! How are you?" He stood up and shook hands with the old man who we all guessed was a Palace annuitant, although we had not set eyes on him before.

At the Palace we honor our pensioners and always make them welcome. They are constantly being urged to drop around and visit the new building. Two years ago the *Palace Voice* started a regular column for annuitants, and told them in an editorial: "To the old-timers who have not yet written we say: 'Please keep in touch! Drop us a line. Remember, your friends are eager to hear about you.'"

This is very nice. The company's kindness-to-annuitants works out well, especially since they hardly ever come around to see us. But today here was Art Blackburn, a former assistant plant-manager, interrupting our conference. Even so, as Mac Tyler said, "the pleasure is all ours, Art. Sit down."

Our visitor, who appeared to be in his early seventies, placed himself in a chair and looked around at us, smiling, without saying anything. His manner was both shy and determined; he drew a sheet of paper from his pocket.

"Sure glad that you could drop by, Art. What brings you to this neck of the woods?" said Mac Tyler.

"Well, stuck off where I am, I don't get a chance to see any of the gang, those that are still left. Nobody comes to see me, so . . . well, it's the first time I've been down in three years."

"You've got to come down more often, Art."

"How can I?" said the annuitant gloomily. "Have they calculated the cost of living lately? I don't guess so. I think twice before I take my car out of the garage. It's not so easy."

"What are you doing with yourself, boy?"

"My legs aren't what they used to be," said Art Blackburn. "The wife has been sick. You know."

"Taking it easy, eh?"

The annuitant made no reply. He was studying the paper in his hand. We waited in silence for him to do something with it. His countenance fell into somber lines, and he said in a toneless voice: "I've got an idea here, and they said over in my old department that you ought to see it. They said you were the man, Mac."

"Well," replied Mac Tyler cheerfully, after a covert glance at his watch. "The boys were right, Art. We're always receptive to new ideas, especially when they come from an experienced hand like yourself."

"It was two weeks ago," said the old man bitterly, no longer paying attention to us, but hoarsely addressing the picture window and the green lawns beyond. "It made my blood boil. This smart aleck. Oh, I admit I haven't kept up. I never see anybody, and after a while you forget some. But there was this young smart aleck from the university—you know, the kind that knows it all, or thinks he does. My wife's cousin Em lives near by, and we went to her house for supper. She has a son in the university who brought along this fellow. Anyhow, when he heard what business I was in, he began making statements such as I wouldn't expect to hear in my lifetime, unless from Bolsheviks. He talked exactly like a Bolshevik about our business."

Indignation widened the old man's eyes. His bitterness was addressed to a larger audience than ours, and a higher authority. He arched his neck as if to discover the shape of what he wanted to say written somewhere beyond the windowpane.

"Naturally I set him straight as best I could. But then he brought up all these college-boy facts and figures that I couldn't—*ten years ago* I would have polished him off! Then this smart aleck said: 'Don't forget, you've been out of things for a while.' Out of things! Well . . . I got out of my chair, but my wife held on to me and they made me sit down.

"It's true enough, you get out of touch when nobody comes around. I thought I'd start a garden, but it gets me in the back. We don't do much, to tell the truth. But if I could have had the ammunition . . ."

Mac Tyler slapped his hand on the table. "Art," he said, "the problem that you describe so well is one we're up against all the time. But what's that idea you were speaking about?"

Our visitor returned his attention to the paper in his hand. "I thought this," he said. "I've drafted a memo on it, which I will leave with you. The idea is, why don't we get up a program to inform the public about our activities—to do away with the general ignorance on the subject?"

It was one of the few times I have seen the chief of the Crystal Palace's public-relations department taken aback. "Well," he said, "I think that's a fine idea, Art. In fact, right now we're trying to mount a major—"

"They told me you'd like it," the old man nodded, and there came into his dim eyes a foxy gleam. "What I want to tell everybody now is that I'm ready to *go to work* on this program in any way I can, the sooner the better. That is, I'm ready and willing—"

"We *know* you are, Art," said Mac Tyler, rising from his chair. "And on behalf of everybody I want to tell you how mightily we appreciate your taking the time to come and visit us, and give us the benefit of your valuable thinking."

"If I could be of some use, is that I mean," said the old man as Mac Tyler pumped his hand. "I'd be willing to come out of . . ."

"You can be certain that we'll remember you, Art, boy; now be sure to come around more often in the future. Do you hear?"

In another minute the mournful annuitant had reached the doorway, and Mac Tyler accompanied him to the corridor. Tyler came back and sat down. "God, isn't that too bad!" he said, and passed his hand quickly in front of his face to wipe away the sad image that had been projected on us. "Those poor guys!" he exclaimed, and we looked at one another.

retirement n. 1. A retiring, or state of being retired: . . .
A withdrawing into seclusion. A withdrawing from office, active service, etc. Secluded condition; privacy.
. . . 2. A place of seclusion.

seclusion n. 1. A secluding; state or fact of being secluded; isolation. 2. A secluded place; a place of retirement.—*Syn.* See SOLITUDE.
                              —*Webster's Collegiate Dictionary*

We play with words and move them around, and soon, I
think, public-relations offices will find a new word for "retirement." This new word will undoubtedly project the
image of continuing activity and participation in life on a
person's own terms, rather than the image of rest (white-
thatched oldster fishing) that we still have before us today.

It may be, I suppose it is, presumptuous on the part of
younger people to tell our senior citizens that the image of
rest is bad for them—that if they think wholly in terms
of rest they will go to pot. No one knows how it feels to be
seventy until he *is* seventy. But this warning comes from the
older men and women themselves. They are the ones who
have told me that for many annuitants who have had their
last buttons pinned on them, had the farewell dinner, had
the president's handshake and their pictures taken for the
Palace Voice, the supposedly green pastures of retirement
can turn out to be a hoax.

The following observations are based on talks with a number of pensioners and my experience as the editor of the Annuitants' Column in the *Palace Voice.* My assignment came
about in this way:

One of our directors who was assigned to the public-relations portfolio, and whose knowledge of this subtle craft was
—273° Centigrade, sought after a few months had gone by to
make a decision of some kind. Almost any decision would do,
so long as he could project it in an authoritative way. But
since public-relations matters escaped him altogether, he was

reduced to okaying Mac Tyler's proposals. These, to be sure, were couched in a humble manner. In the fashion of the true corporation executive, Tyler did his best to transplant the ideas so that they would *seem* to come from the director himself, but this was a courtesy routine and meant nothing.

The director finally came up with his idea, which was that we were woefully neglecting our annuitants' morale. Therefore, we should start an annuitants' column in the paper. A perfectly good public-relations man (myself) was assigned to the project. I didn't care for the job, but in spite of that I found it interesting, and it gave me a greater appreciation of what life was really like for these retired men and women. I read and sorted information from hundreds of their letters to the *Palace Voice*. They came from all kinds of people, since an annuitant can be anyone from an office boy to a retired director. Putting them all together, they reveal a curious patchwork of genuine happiness and misery, renewed purpose and hopeless drifting, complacency and doubt, of regret and unfulfilled dreams, of serenity and a sort of numbness, progressive ill health, and very frequently a growing crankiness and a shriveling-up of isolated and lonely souls.

What is the concept behind our retirement program? It has been called that of "Deferred Reward." Whoever enters the service of the Crystal Palace voluntarily trades in his chances of becoming independent in his youth or early middle age in return for security. His reward, his independence, and opportunity to do as he pleases will come later—when he is sixty-five years old.

To use an earlier analogy, others climb the stairway to success, and they may falter and stumble or take three steps at a time, but they go at their own pace. The corporation man looks the situation over and boards an escalator. The company supplies the moving power. He moves upward at a pace determined by others.

The corporation man forgets any idea of a quick killing, big money (until late in his career), big vacations, or a big reputation. He accepts his position as a middling sort of fellow working at his specialty in comfortable surroundings. He may well receive education and training to deepen his knowledge so that he will advance properly, but always as a member of the team.

The trouble is, you can't retire as a member of the team. When you retire you are *alone*. For the first time in perhaps thirty or forty years you are on your own. This can be a stunning experience. I think it accounts for the strange look on employees' faces when they have service buttons pinned on them. This is a moment of loneliness.

We received a letter from an annuitant who lived in a remote area and had not seen any of his old associates for years, and knew no one with whom he had gone through his business life, and missed it all. Nevertheless he noted wistfully "the wonderful family spirit which exists, and which Walter Ballant (a director) so well expressed in the letter he wrote to me at the time of my retirement: 'You may be sure that there is no possible way in which you can sever your connection with the company or with the friendships you have made in the organization.'"

But there was a possible way, an inevitable way. No doubt the director meant what he said, as we all hopefully do, but the fact remains that our correspondent *had* become completely isolated and had severed all connections with us— except for the pension check and the *Palace Voice,* which described the doings of young men he had never known and must have induced a monthly pang. I can imagine him smoothing out the director's letter and copying its humane message. We in turn would reprint it, and the gentle hoax we play on ourselves would come full circle.

We are all, it seems, saving ourselves for the Senior Prom. But many of us forget that somewhere along the way we must learn to dance. The man whose surroundings are arranged in perfect order by others must make a special effort to exercise his enthusiasm for life. Otherwise he may fall into a state of spiritual flabbiness. This will not matter too much while he is a member of the team, but will render him helpless and unfit to survive as a human being when the supposedly golden day of retirement comes.

Nietzsche made Zarathustra say:

"Alas! There cometh the time when man will no longer launch the arrow of his longing beyond man—and the string of his bow will have unlearned to whizz!

"I tell you: one must still have chaos in one, to give birth to a dancing star. . . ."
and also
"No shepherd, and one herd! Everyone wanteth the same; everyone is equal; he who hath other sentiments goeth voluntarily into the madhouse."

In speaking of Deferred Reward, we venture on uncertain ground. We agree, I am sure, that there is no reward, deferred or not, to be compared with the privilege of having your youth and strength about you. Any concept involving the sacrifice of this youth and strength so that you can finally become your own man at the age of sixty-five would seem to be absurd or fraudulent. Independence is too precious and marvelous a gift to be wasted on the old.

Yet who is independent in his youth? Not many of us. Most young people have to work hard; they are tied down to their jobs and their homes. In fact, insofar as leisure time is concerned, the employees of the Crystal Palace have as much as anyone. And since we don't have brutal competition to contend with, we probably have more strength and peace of mind to enjoy our free time. So what is there to complain about?

It is frustrating to argue oneself into a corner. The letters from our annuitants indicate that there is something questionable about the Deferred Reward idea. Yet for the great majority of people our company's program compares favorably with any other plan for living that has yet been devised. It may be that I am unconsciously reacting against the very fact that it *is* devised. Or perhaps I am objecting to old age itself, and absurdly blaming the corporation for not making available to us the fountain of youth.

One of our sick annuitants confessed ruefully in a letter to the *Voice* (which, of course, we didn't print): "Most of us should have a shot of atomic energy when we retire so that we may be able to enjoy life a few more years than we generally do after retirement."

I have this clip, too, from a trade paper with all names changed:

> "*Prepare Rites for Conrad.* Funeral services were incomplete late today for Eugene Conrad, 63, vice-president of the Matthew Corporation who died at his home early Sunday. By a strange coincidence, he had been honored 36 hours earlier by friends and associates at a testimonial luncheon marking his retirement. . . ."

Needless to say, an item of this kind proves nothing. By choosing our material carefully, we can multiply examples of retiring executives dying in mid-ocean on the first leg of a world cruise, etc. All we can say is that such news items are common enough to suggest that sudden relaxation after years of labor tends to upset the system. More often, however, our annuitants tell us that the main hazard of this relaxation, if prolonged, is that it makes an older person grow stupid before his time.

One correspondent warned: "You will find that unless you keep active you will find yourself slowly turning into a cabbage." Another reported: "Quite an active life and so interesting that it keeps me young and on my feet all the time for which I am glad. We have regular meetings with the other retired people . . . and if I see some of them getting old on account of them doing nothing, I have a feeling that I am better off even if most evenings I may be a little more tired than the others."

What do you bring to retirement? That, it seems, is what you will get out of it. Our letters indicate that the truly blessed quality to take away from the last testimonial dinner is an enthusiasm for life. Like this: "My glads and roses are the talk of the town. Anyone who thinks that things are dull in these little country towns has another think coming. I have more to do now than I ever had—the only difference is that I am now able to do the things I want to do when I want to do them. The day I retired I threw away the alarm clock and tore up the calendar. . . . Organized Little Leaguers, organized Volunteer Ambulance, am treasurer of Fire Department. Retirement is fun and I'm enjoying every minute of it."

But this letter was an exception. It pictures a virtually ideal state of retirement. Few of our correspondents conveyed one tenth of this man's verve. (And how about those who didn't write?) Here are sundry impressions gathered from the letters, notes, and post cards:

The words "puttering" and "taking it easy" recur with

depressing frequency, often with quotation marks around them. Perhaps it is the quotation marks that are depressing. One imagines them accompanied by a diffident shrug of the shoulders. The phrase "taking it easy" conveys everything and nothing. It tells of empty days, one like the other, and desultory hours slipping by, of the meaningless drive in the country, the ritual of listening to the weather report that makes no difference because one is going nowhere, catching fish that one will not eat. And "puttering," what is that? Webster says, an American variant of pottering, which means "to busy oneself with trifles or futilely; trifle or daw-dle (away)."

It seems that we have caught in our language the concept of a potterer as a wasted human being. I have a sudden vision of a vast assemblage of our senior citizens *pottering* from the shuffleboard courts of St. Petersburg to a lonely New England den where an old man is fashioning a ship model, and I see bent figures across the land stooping among sunflowers, radishes, tomato rows, and grapevines, and find myself wanting to shout: "Is this all? Is this what I am saving my money for?"

No sooner do I ask than I know it is a foolish question, for it is up to each man what he will be. The corporation has nothing to do with that. Our company can only be expected to lead me by the hand until the age of sixty-five, and then I must stand on my own. Finally, then. I can, for instance, travel. Like so many of our annuitants, I can buy a trailer and see the country; I can potter across the country. Like some others, I can potter across the whole wide world. Yet in my stubborn and irrational frame of mind, I find this prospect sad too, not because I won't enjoy it in a way, but because I can't enjoy it *now*.

We must work at the Palace for ten years before we become eligible for a three-week vacation. I see our sober-sided young men arriving in their car pools and returning at night to their growing families and their own steeply mortgaged little Crystal Palaces, and then I picture from the letters before me rickety oldsters nodding along the Champs Élysées, peering out of their car windows at the Rhine castles, and old men admiring the lovely girls along the Via Veneto. This vision makes me (I know, unreasonably) furious at the young people who have so trapped themselves in obligations, and who have accepted lock, stock, and barrel the proposition that if they conduct themselves soberly the Deferred Reward will be theirs—in the pottering twilight of life.

For the letters from our annuitants, most of them, reveal that joy long-deferred is a diminished joy. Joy must be *practiced*. The capacity for excitement must be exercised, or when the time comes for you to summon it up it won't be there. Yes, our annuitant travelers, like most old people, appear to enjoy scenery very much. They enjoy renewing the acquaintance of old associates who have settled in far-off places. But apart from the scenery and these occasional "cutting up old touches with the Bill Smiths" and "we spent a pleasant day and night reminiscing with the Eliot Wheelocks," our correspondents seem hardly aware that they are away from home. The impact of new people, architecture, and the living history of a strange land that so often rocks and moves and excites a younger visitor simply cannot excite an old traveler in the same way unless he has kept alive and open for adventure during all his young years.

And how hard it is for the majority of corporation men (at least the ones I know) to feel adventurous. Insulated from life as we are by the daily round in our thermos-bottle organization, hedged in by a network of benefits and obligations, and above all, *seduced*—there is no other word—by the growing pile of savings that one dares not take and use for purposes of joy, but must save for the pottering years, most of us become docile and unimaginative long before we reach sixty-five.

What manner of man is this, his hour come at last, who shuffles toward his rose garden, waiting to be born? In fact, the garden is the place where a great many of our annuitants find solace. They write, often movingly, of the joys of gardening. They teach us that when we are old, even if the heart has no other place to go, we can devote ourselves to nature and celebrate its smaller cycles, and take heart from the budding and flowering of what we have planted. I think this is a sort of rebirth. From their letters it seems to me that the annuitants' preoccupation with gardening represents at once a giving up of life and a rejoining of it in a new way. Few of our still-active pensioners who have gone into business for themselves mention their flower beds. But those who appear to have resigned from the human race are the ones you will see moving about their gardens with smiles and trembling steps before nightfall.

We are advised also that in order to avoid vegetating in retirement we ought in our middle years to develop a hobby or two. Then, once the savor has gone out of our days we can turn to the old stamp album. We can braid leather belts. We can board an electric cart and swat around the golf course, or take up photography and snap pictures of our grandchildren in every possible pose of youth.

I think a hobby is only as good as the imagination that directs it. Conceived as a distraction from work, snapping photos of one's grandchildren may be a pleasing way to spend a weekend. But when there is no other work and the hobby stands alone, an endless series of snapshots begins after a while to pall. The Brownie will soon lie idle if the hobby-ist does not frame his pursuit within a sense of art, and of life passing, of history perhaps—the point is that the hobby must mean something.

Hence, what must develop in a man and woman, in youth and middle years, is not merely a talent for distracting oneself but a talent for living, a *concern* with what goes on. It will be this concern as it is invested in the hobby that will make it satisfying or not.

I wonder whether the life we lead at the Crystal Palace doesn't tend to remove *concern* from our hearts. Again, heaven knows, it is not the company's fault. The Palace gives every opportunity to souls within its walls to develop as they will. The way of life we have accepted asks only one thing of us—that we postpone our dreams for forty years.

Is that asking too much? A mere forty years . . . they will slip by like nothing at all. No dreams—no worries. That's a fair exchange. "Done!" we say, and from that time forward the twenty-five-year-old boy with the crew cut and the honest face prepares to become an old man. The life insurance, the savings, the electronic properties on the installment plan, the modest demeanor, the cooperative reflexes, the voluntary subjection of temperament, the wise and temperate restrictions of desire, are all, all preparations for the brief twilight of a gracious old age.

But for the young man with a crew cut, even with all these things going for him, there is not the slightest guarantee that his old age will be a golden time. For one it can be golden, for another, lonely and miserable and sick, *quite apart* from the amount of money invested in it. True, it is far better for an annuitant to be comfortably fixed than living off his social security and a few pinched dollars. But what guarantee can there be that he will, physically, remain in condition to enjoy the savings he has accumulated through the years of "sensible" self-denial? Age may turn out to be liver trouble, creaky legs, and having to get up in the night; it is generally incapacity of one kind or another, and you can't buy forty again. You can't even buy fifty and fifty-five. Finally, you can't buy memories of the trip you didn't take, the adventure you declined, the struggle you by-passed, the excitement you had no eyes to see. These memories are the coins of the spirit. They can make a seventy-year-old man so rich in held-onto youth that he can truly say that life has just begun for him. Without such memories he will be desperately poor in spirit. And that is a form of poverty not covered by any insurance program, and which may in fact be *induced* by a program that fosters a lifetime of smug self-denial.

If every annuitant could know in advance, in T. S. Eliot's lines from *Burnt Norton,* that:

> *"What might have been and what has been*
> *Point to one end, which is always present.*
> *Footfalls echo in the memory*
> *Down the passage which we did not take*
> *Towards the door we never opened*
> *Into the rose-garden. . . ."*

I think again of the sad letter to the *Palace Voice:*

"Most of us should have a shot of atomic energy when we retire so that we may be able to enjoy life a few more years than we generally do after retirement."

Compare this with:

"Busy ranching six months—raising horses, cattle . . . close ranch after hunting season (wild turkey, deer, grouse) . . . winter in village of N—where I am chairman of the Village Council and at times Acting Mayor.

". . . Winter activities—studying Spanish, operating small green house and making Spanish Colonial furniture."

Both of these men served long and honorable years in our company. Four decades ago they were young and hard-muscled, and looking ahead. One retained a controlling interest over his spirit; the other buried himself in the organization. Now they have gone to their Deferred Reward. The first is so impatiently busy that he can barely take the time to scribble his card. The second craves a final boon from the company—a shot of atomic energy. Thus, the man who thinks that the savings plan will take care of everything potters at the end of the rainbow.

XII. *I Believe What Is Absurd*

We must believe in the worthwhileness of a job or suffer stress, or lapse into an amiable or sullen not-caring. Most business enterprises have to take into account the problem of belief where middle-level employees are concerned. At lower levels where subsistence is the main worry "belief in your job" couldn't matter less. It would be fantastic for a restaurant dishwasher to "believe" in his work. Important though his labor may be in terms of public health, any dishwasher who has a chance to escape to a higher skill will do so.

But the higher we rise in skill and salary the more closely we look at the meaning and importance of what we do for a living. I think the need for us to believe in *something* in relation to our jobs can't be overestimated. You must take some kind of attitude toward your work. Every salaried person I have ever known, within and outside of the Crystal Palace, has made some effort to rationalize, justify, account for himself. The bitter, negative form of the question is "What's your excuse?" The positive if sometimes unspoken answer frames itself within the idea: "What I am doing is good, because . . ."

I don't mean to say that we encounter windily articulate

credos among business people—except in public speeches, employee pamphlets, and philosophical business magazines. You don't hear salesmen singing "I Believe . . ." For most of us, commercial belief is a small rock, a reference point on the landscape . . . yet it must be there or we will lose our bearings.

Imagine a company, created by the whim of a rich man's will, whose sole function was to dig holes in the ground and fill them up again, and then smooth over the scarred earth so that not a trace of the ridiculous operation would remain. How many self-respecting employees would stay with such a firm over a long period? I don't know, but I would guess, for example, that the bulldozer operator—no matter how well paid—would eventually quit such an assignment for the simple reason that it insulted him as a human being.

(This digging and refilling of holes is an ancient form of punishment in the army, and is intended as an insult to incompetent or unruly soldiers. The premise: "You have conducted yourselves in sub-human fashion. Therefore, you will be treated as sub-human beings until you get on the ball.")

Among salaried people, what beliefs are possible? We may, I think, believe in (1) a product (2) making money (3) getting ahead (4) being "a pro" (5) sheer process, and in (6) the company itself. Taking them in order:

I believe in our product. The highest and most satisfying form of commercial belief is the conviction that the product I am working for is essential, or at least helpful, to mankind. If I can't have that, I should be able to assume, at any rate, that our product is the best of its kind on the market. Lacking that, let me have faith that it is not positively the worst of its kind. Take even that way, and please assure me that it is not poisonous. Without such an assurance, I will have to justify my job in another way.

Most companies today are acutely conscious of the need to explain to their employees as well as to the public that the products they sell are beneficial to society. Before we start on a job we are usually asked for some kind of affirmation. We have to state our attitude. At times the setting forth of a graceful and proper statement can be a problem in itself.

Shortly after World War II I followed a lead to a cough-drop company. I was stopped on the telephone by the personnel manager's question: "Why do you want to come with us?"

"What was that, sir?"

"What is there about our company that attracts you to us?"

I stalled and improvised in all directions, but couldn't think of anything to say about cough drops. What attracted me to the company was that it had a job open, and I needed the money. Time enough later to learn their catechism. I would *credo* in cough medicine as soon as my first pay check arrived. Finally (lying, of course, since this simulated-stress method, as we have seen, elicits fantasies), I went on about the company's great name and was accepted for the interview.

Later, after negotiating the obstacle course all the way to the vice-president, I came acropper before a perceptive man. In my defense I must say that the earlier tests, which I passed, had made me extremely nervous. The unnerving began in the first minute of my first interview when the personnel fellow snapped: "Why does your left eye deviate when you look at me?"

I said: "I guess it's because I've always had a weak muscle in my left eye. Sometimes it wanders, but usually I can control it."

He regarded me happily. "Good! You weren't embarrassed!" he said, and wrote something down. I had made a friend, and he shepherded me through the sales and advertising managers, and the psychiatrist. I was very good. I had even noticed in the paper, by some fluke, that the assistant sales manager was entered in a hole-in-one tournament, and mentioned it to him. I made but one mistake during this passage. With a growing bomb of pressure inside of me I said that I had once written copy for the Drock Blug Company, instead of Block Drug, but this, too, redounded to my credit because I made a good, laughing recovery from the slip.

"You weren't embarrassed!" chuckled my friend, rubbing his hands. "That's all-important, you know." Meanwhile I had passed the psychological test. But twenty-four hours later the remarkable vice-president discovered a weakness that the others had missed.

He did it by hinting in a confidential way that the company's products were not as good as advertised. "That won't bother you, will it?" he laughed. I sensed a trap, and replied that I was sure they were excellent, the best. I believed in them. "Well, that's fine," he said, "but that won't bother you, will it?" What I should have done, I realize now, was to look him undeviatingly in the eye and say that I didn't feel like knocking down a product I wanted to work for. This would be a statement of principle that I *believed in believing*, which is sophisticated, rather than a statement of actually believing, which, if you follow me, *he* couldn't believe. Or perhaps to this day I haven't figured it out— damn these simulated stress interviews!

His apparently black cynicism regarding cough drops confused me utterly. I moved in gingerly fashion around this porcupine of Belief, possibly betraying the fact that I cared too much about it.

Next morning I received a call from my friend, the personnel man. He was dejected and bewildered. The vice-president had turned me down. "I don't get it," my shepherd said unhappily, "but Mr. Pomfret says that you're going to write a book. I assured him positively that you weren't, but he has the last word around here."

At the Crystal Palace we have the spiritual luxury of a fine line of products. Without question they make life easier and healthier for everyone, and if suddenly withdrawn from the community they would be missed. Therefore, we can easily believe in our products. We may be said to have product-loyalty; we can respect our common effort, which is ultimately to distribute our brands and sell as many units as we can. On the other hand, I find it hard to *credo* in a distribution effort. I know that somewhere back in a laboratory our brands are being tested, developed, and improved. I know that somewhere out there in the great public world beyond headquarters our products are being sold. But from where I sit within the Crystal Palace's administrative solar system the product seems as far away as Uranus. I gaze into a commercial infinity in which no product appears important.

Instead of a rock on which I can found my belief, I see thousands of pebbles whirling in clusters about our system, each one equally insignificant. I am aware that our brands are "good," but my part in our huge system is so small that I can't relate to the product.

The old-style commission salesman could work up a belief in his pots and pans because he handled them personally. He touched them and felt their shine; he observed how the customers liked them; he heard the cash register jingle, and the more it jingled the more recognition he received via his lustrous hardware. We administrative teamworkers enjoy no such satisfaction. Collectively remote from the product, rewarded collectively in a good year, we are not lost but simply turning in our administrative orbits—not miserable, not complaining, just there. For this reason the corporation-employee's belief in the company product is generally not a powerful image; it is not his rock. Rather it provides us with a vague over-all sense of righteousness. We trust that we are involved in a good thing. We are, as Pascal said, a mean between two infinite extremes, taking what spiritual nourishment we can from the knowledge that our infinity appears to be moving in the right direction.

But I am continually troubled by the insignificance of my efforts on behalf of the Crystal Palace products. It is absurd to have faith in an effort that doesn't need me. If I should vanish behind the locks of our atomic bomb shelter the company wouldn't sell *one unit less*. It isn't that the company fails to appreciate my work. In his Christmas message the president always makes the point that nothing could have been accomplished in the past year without the loyal cooperation of every individual man and woman in the organization doing his and her part. These messages are good and heartening, and they have twice given me added satisfaction in that I wrote them myself.

However mightily indoctrination teams labor to convince employees of the importance of cough drops, chewing gum, and toothpaste in the general scheme of things, the fact is that they are trivial products. We could easily get along without them. (You can brush your teeth with salt or baking soda.) Hence, anyone devoting his life to the promotion of these items comes—in terms of a philosophical accounting for himself—bang up against a double absurdity. Should he really manage to believe that his brand of cough drops offers any great and lasting benefit to people with sore throats, or even that his brand is markedly superior to all competitive brands (which may contain virtually the same soothing and lubricative ingredients), he takes a foolish position. But equally, if he does *not* believe in the product he is pushing, his entire working day from morning to night becomes an unrelieved exercise in dishonesty.

The fool has always been absurd in the eyes of man; the knave, in the eyes of God. The fool could die in bed without discovering the ignobility of his cough drop. Not so the knave—he chuckled all the way to the grave at the gullibility of his customers. Today things have changed. An evangelism has entered American commercial life. It has all but done away with the fool and, for the first time, made the dishonest man's position absurd. Today the fool and knave are as one.

The new evangelism, whether expressed in soft or hard selling, is a quasi-religious approach to business wrapped in a hoax—a hoax voluntarily entered into by producers and consumers together. Its credo is that of *belief-to-order*. It is the truth-to-order as delivered by advertising and public relations men, believed by them, and voluntarily believed in by the public. Fragments of this strange process of deliberate self-deception have been caricatured as "sincerity."

A few years ago one of television's most sincere salesmen was reported to be squabbling with his sponsor, Dover Cigarettes. Network officials were unhappily caught in the middle. Newspaper reporters crowded them with all sorts of embarrassing questions. The salesman, call him Len Bosworth, was apparently being difficult. This extract from a press interview (with names changed) was printed in a national magazine:

"How about the rumor that Bosworth was giving up smoking? Network spokesman: 'If he said that, it was probably a joke. I can't believe that Len would be that rude to a personal friend like Carlson Kenworthy, the Dover president.' "

That exchange, it seems to me, captures a set of extraordinary assumptions—all the more extraordinary because they have become commonplace. First, that it can possibly be rude for a man to give up smoking! The speaker does not consider the possibility of a doctor advising someone to quit cigarettes, or of the man himself deciding that he felt better without them. Why does the speaker not entertain this thought—at least at the moment the question is put to him? Possibly for the reason that the broadcasting network he represents is deeply involved with the cigarette, and beams the cigarette's "sincere" message, which must be "true" or the network would not carry it. Since the message is "true," all of us intimately involved in broadcasting and telecasting it must believe-to-order in what it says. Otherwise we will be dishonest. Worse still, the truth will become dishonest. It is rude to affront the truth with insulting facts.

I have no idea, and it is none of our business, whether Len Bosworth ever seriously planned to give up smoking. Supposing he did contemplate it, however, a terribly embarrassing situation is created. Bosworth, a pioneer in sincerity, has presumably enjoyed cigarettes for many years. The unstated but strong implication of the commercials he reads or ad libs is not only that smoking gives him and all of us a deep pleasure, but also that (to repeat, unstated) each inhalation of joy is *harmless*. But all of a sudden, it is rumored, the star is going to quit this harmless joy. Impossible! "If he said that, it was probably a joke." A disturbing joke. A few more like that, and—

At any rate, the commotion surrounding Bosworth's smoking or not smoking takes place within this fabulous truth-to-order world of commercial sincerity, a world created by voluntary hoax, as if we had enclosed ourselves within a transparent balloon and called it the universe, pointing upward and saying: "There! The truth goes so far and no farther. Within this balloon (and nothing that matters exists outside of it) Bosworth smokes." Do we not trap poor Bosworth himself in our illusion?

But, astoundingly enough, everyone within the balloon really knows that the star is being paid to extol the product, and that he wouldn't praise it, and perhaps wouldn't even smoke it, if the money were not forthcoming. Still, it would be rude of the star to break not the illusion but the pretended illusion.

On a primitive level we see the same curious voluntary self-deception in wrestling exhibitions. Wrestling fans become sincerely furious at a bald-headed villain seeming to foul the hero, even when they know he isn't doing any such thing. If the police were not on guard, the crowd would be capable of sincerely lynching Skull Smith, or whoever, and pleading innocent on the grounds that his *performance* had made retribution inevitable.

What on earth then is one to believe about Belief? Belief and Make-Believe seem to have merged. There was a time, for example, when all radio and TV announcers read commercials, and that was that. Usually they pitched their voices a little differently during the read-for-pay message. Clearly the voice was hired; the voice was a vehicle. Even the sideshow barker who pretended to believe in the wonders within the tent was not putting his very soul into his pitch. But with the advent of the new evangelism, pitchmen involve *themselves* in the product, and by means of some peculiar convolution through which we have been able to make our minds stand on their heads, we agree to pretend to think that they really care; whereupon, in response to our fakery, they *do* care—and if that sounds mixed up, it is, and we are.

Voluntary self-deception, of course, is as old as the fable of the Emperor who had no clothes on. We find the temporarily self-deceiving salesman in Chaucer's Pardoner. But the Emperor's subjects were mystified by fear, and the Pardoner's belief in his worthless relics was emotional and quickly challenged by his listeners.

This commercial hoax of ours has become a veritable, so to speak, fact of life for millions of people. Our absurdity is taken as a matter of course; it might be said that we make a virtue of absurdity. And those who question it are put in the position of being hopelessly naïve.

I remember having to believe in a certain cigarette lighter. It was always running out of fluid, which was my fault, so I kept matches handy. At the lighter-company's plant I surreptitiously lit a match. The agency account executive saw me and almost lost his mind. I can understand that, for it was rude to light my cigarette with a match in these surroundings. That Christmas I received a very good lighter made by a rival company. Naturally I could never use it. Absurd? Yes, but equally so if I *had* used it and continued to celebrate and make my living from our product.

Credo, credo . . . perhaps without realizing it we have interpreted Einstein's vision in a certain way to permit the mobility of truth. A patronizing view would be that the masses have discovered that truth is utterly mobile and relative; that there is your truth and mine, the truth of Camels and the truth of Chesterfields, and who is to say which is valid? Truth has become democratic. Everybody has one vote.

From there we can go on to the proposition that since nothing is absolutely true, anything *may* be true. And if anything may be true, if you think hard enough it only takes a little emotional conviction to make it so. Moreover our mobile truth has done away with dishonesty. It permits even fraudulent people to manufacture sincere belief in what they are doing.

The cherished rock of belief turns out to be a portable rock; you carry it around with you and set it down where you please. I believe in my product, but give me some more money and I'll believe in yours . . . and people won't blame me. Why should they? We are all in this hoax together.

There still ought to be a commercial belief existing somewhere beyond the confines of our balloon. I am salaried and there is a product involved in my work, but it does not satisfy me spiritually. Well then, perhaps . . .

I believe in making money. Money is the coin of manhood. It measures the length and strength of my manhood. It is the skin of the dangerous leopard, the bacon from the wily pig that I bring home because I am strong and know my way around our forest. If you haven't made much money, according to the reasoning of our tribe, it means that you haven't figured out the forest very well. You don't know the right paths. Your stalking tactics are inadequate. You don't know a bear from a boar, and throw your spear at the wrong game. Deep inside of you, perhaps, you don't care for the hunt. The question of your courage may arise, and the question of adequacy.

Why should I not believe in money? The possession of money makes men more masculine and women more feminine. Cash enlarges the soul. Money creates beauty where there was none before. It is positively erotic and can buy gaiety. When I have money I am a much nicer person, tolerant, kind and understanding, and I forgive the sins of others. I give to charity and feel better. Without money I become mean-spirited, pinched and envious, and resentful of others' good fortune.

Yet a belief in making money, by itself, for some reason has little spiritual appeal. It won't do for me, partly because I suspect that I will never pile up a great amount. If money is the top, and I believe in it, then I will be inferior to too many people. Also one hundred dollar bills are not really mine to do with as I like. They belong to the country. I can't burn them or I will go to jail. If I stand on the street corner and distribute them to passers-by I will be locked up. (But if I gave away apples I would merely be told to move on.)

We need not labor the point that money is an end in itself only for sick souls, misers. The rest of us use it to obtain something else, like food or phonograph records. Someone with absolutely no interest in life but money is poverty-stricken and invariably miserable. He can buy people, of course, but what are you going to do with people once you have them, unless you maintain outside values? You must talk with them (about something), dance with them, sleep with them, go bowling with them.

No, money in itself will not do as an object of belief. It serves rather to foster other aims. At the Crystal Palace most of us employ money to build a wall of greenbacks around our lives. Money is our Maginot Line against the invasion of old age that will surely take place a few decades from now. I have known men who wielded dollar bills as if they were hand grenades; others use them to bait traps, still others make toy planes out of them and sail them through the air to earn a laugh. What these three are saying is: "I believe

in war," "I believe in trickery," and "I believe in laughs."
But they are trivial credos. We are speaking of a deeper
reason-why.

I believe in getting ahead. More and more, commercial
status is becoming a substitute for money. Status—that is to
say, what others think I am—is not taxable. I want the world
to smile at me approvingly and say: "There's a man who's
getting ahead." Never mind what I am getting ahead *at*.
That is unimportant. All you have to do is look into my
garage and see how many cars you find there. Care to check
my insurance coverage? I dare say you will find it in apple-
pie order. Come see us at your earliest opportunity, but
hurry because we are moving to a new home in a slightly
better neighborhood. We sort of outgrew our old place after
my last promotion. What am I looking forward to? Just this:
some day on my gravestone may it be written: "He Got
Ahead."

No, it is wrong and far too easy to mock this sort of thing.
Of all absurdities, I think, the simple, trusting faith in status
and "aheadness" as an absolute value represents the most
pathetic misunderstanding of what life is about.

There is a form of mental illness in which the patient
suffers from a touch syndrome. Wherever he goes, from room
to room and place to place, he is compelled to touch things,
hold things in his hand, and continually jangle, twirl,
weigh, and measure inanimate objects in order to relate to
his surroundings. Thus it is with the family whose religion
is "getting ahead." They must always have props in order to
prove where they are. They must measure their progress by
the size and cost of the facilities they can buy. The administrative functionary graduates from a brown-leather couch to
a red-leather couch in his office. Or he graduates from one
kind of car to another.

These are clichés, but we are looking into a style of living that is precisely one long cliché, and have you ever noticed what a joyless way of living it can be? Last year I visited a family in a top suburb, and the master of the house, an intelligent and nice man, conducted me through every room of his newly acquired and newly furnished home. He listed the value and make of every article of furniture, of every wall-hanging, bedspread, and inner-spring mattress, and the hi-fi set, and this, and that. He brushed his hand over all these possessions, *felt* them, yet we never paused in our tour. I had the impression that he didn't actually enjoy any of these things. Why? Because as soon as they were outmoded by two or three years they would be replaced by some newer and more fashionable make. Everything he owned seemed to be in motion, and in the process of becoming obsolescent at the very moment it was installed. He turned on the hi-fi set, and jumped from station to station, then put on one record with massed violins and another that blared forth the sound of a thousand bassoons, switched it off, knocked on the walnut paneling, opened a panel and shut it, rolled aside a secret liquor closet, shut that, pressed a switch that slid the phonograph back into the wall. We moved on past blenders and automatic washers and dryers (which he turned on and off), fetched up suddenly in the garage, rolled up the doors by remote control . . . it was too much. He was, literally, a man possessed.

He could speak of nothing but his possessions. I know that if these plastic, electronic, and textile symbols ever cease to pass through his house, if they should somehow mysteriously vanish, this family, these good people, will be frozen in terror on an empty plateau. They will have no belief to console them, no rock, no promontory of faith, and certainly no place to hide in the pitiful wastes of their vulgarity.

I recently bought a big television set in first class condition, less than a year old, for sixty dollars. This was possible because I have an acquaintance who cannot bear to own anything that is even slightly outmoded. As soon as a new and improved product reaches the market he must frantically unload the set or appliance he has, get it out of the house immediately, and buy the latest. He is a caricature, an unbelievably *avant-garde* consumer, but he has done no more than carry the "getting ahead" religion (in terms of consuming things) all the way. Clearly, I think, there is no relief or belief for us along this road.

I believe in being a pro. A pro, said Humphrey Bogart, is someone who does his job well whether he feels like it or not. True, and of course he is many other things besides. We must say immediately that he is always a valuable person. We need his skill, and will pay for it. Give him the job at hand, and relax. He has done it hundreds of times before. We may be sure that this time, as always, he will give us full value.

The worth of a professional may be more accurately fixed than that of non-specialists. In one way this is an advantage for him; in another, a limitation. The vague talents of an "official" may earn him a reward out of all proportion to the value of his services. We don't know exactly what he has done, but since our enterprise seems to be doing well enough we suppose that he must have been administratively responsible for the results we have—and we pay for what we trust he accomplished. But we can generally *see* what a professional has accomplished. His achievement is clear, well-outlined, and self-limiting. We pay him for what he has done, and nothing else.

The solid professional is a credit to the human race. How pleasing to watch him in action! The benevolent, grandfatherly face of the locomotive engineer looking down on the passengers as they hurry past his black cabin at the end of a run; the seventy-eighth violinist, lost in the big orchestra, bowing, a lock of hair swaying across his forehead, his alert black eyes on the conductor; the harbor pilot ascending with heavy grace to the bridge as lesser sailors make way for him; the engineer, thumbs hooked around his belt, squinting at the blueprint I can't read; the tough hack newspaperman who has seen it all, more or less, looking at you with the cigarette hung out of his mouth, just like the movies, as you approach his desk—all pro's! Wonderful people! No wonder we aspire to these high skills. They give a man dignity.

Professionalism also affords us the best excuse in the world for not believing in anything but craftsmanship. In the absence of a genuine philosophical goal, the satisfaction of functioning as a respected pro is next best. In some professional circles, moreover, it is considered naïve and boy-scoutish to have a philosophical orientation, or to believe in anything. There has come into being the Cult of the Pro. The pro does his job, that's all . . . understand? The professional pro likes to think of himself as above belief. A crack specialist, he carries out his assignments proudly not giving a damn for the reasons why or the consequences.

During the early years of World War II, some months before Pearl Harbor, an editorial writer was "exposed" by a gleeful competitor for an apparent inconsistency in his approach to the war. For his newspaper he wrote pro-isolationist editorials insisting that the American people stay out of European quarrels. But for a magazine he wrote equally powerful editorials urging America to help save the Western Allies, even at the risk of war. Here we had one writer putting his talents to work for two fiercely opposed causes—for money. We had a real pro if there ever was one.

Did the exposé bother him? Not in the least. He appeared honestly amazed that anyone would think twice about what he had done. He explained that he was a pro. This was the equivalent of a license enabling a man to abandon moral responsibility. It put him in the position, it legalized his position, of being a moral moron. The issue of war or peace was not great enough to engage the "here I stand" convictions of this sophisticated man.

At the Crystal Palace our professionals seldom have to balance a moral choice of that kind. They are in the main efficiency men of one sort or another. Their most common challenge will be one to determine how far they can go in politely resisting seemingly impractical instructions from a superior official. But we are taught to assume that in an organization as huge as ours no one individual can hope to comprehend the larger picture. If higher authority has arrived at a certain decree we try to understand that our superiors have had access to information that we know nothing about. (Such as the fact that a member of the board of directors has placed his fist gently on the table and said: "I suggest that you do it this way.") So our specialists make do with the conditions that prevail.

The pure pro may avoid absurdity by retreating into his skill and refusing to venture beyond its borders. In his own sphere he remains morally clean. But in addressing himself solely to technical matters he has in effect abdicated his moral sovereignty over the events taking place around him. "I do my job," he says, "that's all I care about." Yet there are times when even he is not permitted to escape our marvelous schizophrenia.

Several months ago a good friend, an engineer in a medium-sized corporation, told me this story. A brother engineer at the same plant had quit his job two years before. He had been unhappy in his work and wanted to study architecture. Following his dream he had done post-graduate work and taken a meagerly paid job as a university assistant. He and his bride had to scrimp, but they were happy. He poured his energies into obtaining a Ph.D., and before long would have it in his pocket.

Back at the plant it turned out that the former engineer was sorely missed. He had a number of rare skills that were not easily to be found. My friend was dispatched to the campus to bring him back to the company. The lure would be a big, handsome salary—two or three times what the university could afford to pay a struggling architect.

"I'm going there tomorrow," my friend said. "I'm going to do everything I can to make him come back to us—and for his sake I hope he resists me. I hope he realizes that from his point of view I am Satan."

Isn't this new? A decent man, self-confessedly appearing before his old associate as a messenger from Satan, perfectly split, simultaneously hoping that his mission (a) would, and (b) would not be successful! My friend, to repeat, *is* a decent person, but he is also an engineer, and beyond that a pro. You cannot say that he lacks humanity, for his role saddened him and he outlined in a most sensitive way the agonizing decision that would be put up to the poor architect. Yet the engineering of temptation had, for professional reasons, to be tried, and my friend was going to give it everything in his repertoire.

The story has a pleasant ending. The architect resisted the company's blandishments, and no one was happier about the whole thing than Satan's emissary.

But does not this remorseless "sincerity" of ours make strange demands on us? It seems that a sophisticated businessman, if he is not to go out of his mind, must maintain a split-level personality. "Lord I believe; help thou mine unbelief." Not any more. Today we ask: "Lord, help me to believe two things at once."

For years I was puzzled by a news item that told of a high official in a soft-drink company moving over to a top position with that company's major rival. Say he moved from A-Cola to B-Cola. This bothered me because I knew another important man in A-Cola who believed-to-order in his product to such an extent that he had a refrigerated drawer in his desk and would offer all visitors a bottle of his harmless potion. He was curiously enough a sardonic individual, but on this level he was split-serious. Once at a party I offered him a cool, glistening glass of the rival drink—the only cola mixer in the house—and he unsmilingly declined. Now . . . how in the world, I wondered, can such a man (I am making a jump and supposing that the official of the news item split-believed as seriously as my acquaintance) switch even this ersatz type of loyalty without embarrassment? What goes on in his mind? Are his taste buds altered in some psychosomatic fashion to respond to the drink he formerly despised? Thinking it over, perhaps I understand what his explanation would be.

I believe in sheer process. This is akin to being a pro, but slightly different. The professional takes refuge in his craft; the efficiency man reverses an old maxim and declares that the means justify the end. For him ends hardly matter at all. At press conferences he has more than once told respectful newsmen: "I believe in production." He may be speaking of rabbits, soft drinks, or automobiles. It doesn't make any difference. Long ago he decided that process is an end in itself. In his last oxygen tent he will cry out: "Production and more production!"

I think that those who believe in process are driven by a

peculiar aesthetic sense. They delight in symmetry and system, the dovetailing of parts, and the blending of work-flows throughout an organization. I have seen a man go into a sort of ecstasy over a new filing and communications system. The process itself filled him with excitement. In a talk before a national management group, he explained:

> "My paperwork experience to date leads me to suggest that the basic approach to the paperwork problem, as to so many other problems, is *control.* Effective control requires a specialist—an expert who can operate from the broad viewpoint. . . . This is where I entered the picture, with broad authority to move in on all fronts to bring paperwork under control and keep it there.
>
> "Once there was someone to exercise control, the next step was setting up the control system. This leads us to the heart of our paperwork system: our communications code. In order to control the flow, storage, and retrieval of paper and the information it contains, we decided to create a coding system which would classify each piece of paper introduced into our communications network. In short, each paper would require a 'license number' before being permitted to travel. . . ." etc.

I think the speaker is conveying to his audience a low-grade aesthetic experience. The rituals of administration, the sterile orderliness of interlocking forms, move him to eloquence. Papers flowing through their proper channels, attended by a guard of immaculate numbers, charm him with an endless and delightful ceremony.

On the cover of his printed speech appears this quotation: "Paperwork can be handled more efficiently when the office is recognized as a *function* rather than as a *place*." Authors of this quote are Charles B. Hicks and, coincidentally, Irene Place. I suspect that they are going too far. Sheer process is fine, but it must be recognized as occurring in some theater, some earthbound milieu, or the whole concept will shoot off into an imaginary realm of space that has nothing to do with our reality. After all, someone at the Crystal Palace did put that open ketchup bottle in the communication tubes. That sort of thing never happens in a function, but occasionally does in a place. In a place, also, employees may become bored with their routine and spend too much time in the ladies room or at the coffee wagon, and might even, in a moment of rage, *tear up* or deliberately lose correspondence—a most unfunctional but conceivable occurrence that should be taken into account.

The main trouble with believing in sheer process is that this obsession includes humanity within procedure. The dedicated production man loses himself in the fascinating mathematics of delivering goods efficiently from the factory to us. This is a fine occupation, but once he begins to *credo* in logistics and throw his being into it, he can turn, spiritually, into a man in an attic playing endlessly with toy trains. It is easy for him to lose all interest in other people, except insofar as they are effective instruments in his game. The true believer in process generally becomes unpopular and lonely, one of those sniff-nosed efficiency types whom everybody fears and abhors. He can stand that no doubt. Anyone grimly devoted to process probably never cared too much for others in the first place. But process, finally, at two o'clock in the morning is a cheerless object of belief because it has no warmth, no human reference, and no objective other than its own continuation. Must we be reduced to believing in a production line or a filing system?

More than a quarter-century ago José Ortega y Gasset wrote in *The Revolt of the Masses*:

"Human life, by its very nature, has to be dedicated to something, an enterprise glorious or humble, a destiny illustrious or trivial. . . . If that life of mine, which concerns only myself, is not directed by me towards something, it will be disjointed, lacking in tension and in 'form.' In these years we are witnessing the gigantic spectacle of innumerable human lives wandering about lost in their own labyrinths, through not having anything to which to give themselves."

If I am one of these innumerable wanderers in the world of business, is there not something for me to believe in? May there be one more possible *credo* for me? I think so.

I believe in our company. We have strayed a long way from the Crystal Palace, but by a circuitous route we now return. For if I am lost in the split-level values of modern business, the High Corporation will serve as my High Church. Like the church, my Crystal Palace removes the burden of belief from me. It removes my need for decision. I have found my rock. I only believe in the company.

Like the church, our company is good and wise. In the context of business enterprise, it is the inheritor and vessel of a mighty tradition. Our company has achieved high ethics and kindness, and cares for me, and will see me through to sixty-five, and send me checks after that. Church and Palace alike are sanctuaries in the jungle of unbridled competition. At the head of the church is God. On the top floor of the Crystal Palace . . . it doesn't matter, since I will never arrive there.

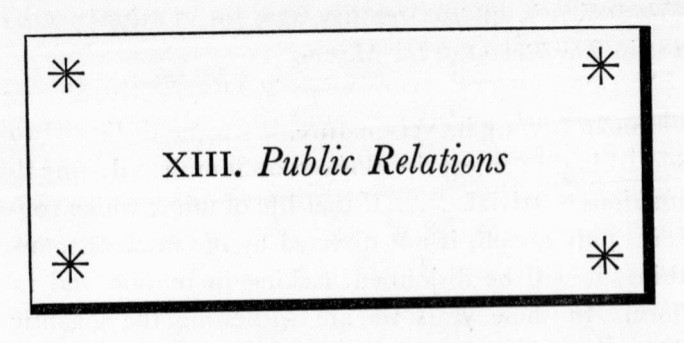

XIII. *Public Relations*

There are a million definitions of public relations. I have found it to be the craft of arranging truths so that people will like you. Public-relations specialists make flower arrangements of the facts, placing them so that the wilted and less attractive petals are hidden by sturdy blooms. Public relations almost invariably involve altering the truth in a nice way, if only by withholding unpleasant news. The PR man may tell the truth and nothing but the truth, but he seldom aims at telling the whole truth. If you were concerned with the unvarnished truth, you wouldn't need a public-relations man at all. A plain information service would do the job. Therefore, in public relations, our aim—however thin you slice it—is to distort, our *raison d'être* is to select and distort the facts in such a way that our clients will appear before the public in a good light. This could, severely, be called the art, science, skill, dodge or trade of lying.

But that judgment would be unfair. A reputable PR practitioner never deliberately lies. Rather he sees before him a world of mobile and malleable truths. A ball of wax is a ball of wax. You can apply heat to it and freeze it, and twist it into peculiar shapes, but it's still wax, isn't it? It is the same material you started out with—shaped a bit.

In the world of public relations, facts can be shaped with no damage to anyone's conscience.

The client of a PR man I know was concerned indirectly with a national plowing contest. The company had subsidized the plowman from, say, Arcadia, with the hope that he would do well and that the corporation would share in a bit of his glory, thereby winning new friends in its Arcadia territory. The plowboy was escorted about the city; executives had their pictures taken with him, etc. Unfortunately, a few days later he came in *last* in a field of fifty entrants. The PR man charged with reporting the event to Arcadia newspapers had of course to "arrange" this lamentable fact. The task didn't phase him for a moment. His news release began something like this: "A tribute to Arcadia's fertile and stone-free soil was written under flaming skies at Lonely Gulch, Iowa today. . . ." The story went on to explain that the boy from Arcadia had never before encountered such rough conditions. It was to be expected that plowmen from bitter hard-earth areas where the soil was pitifully inferior to that of Arcadia would make a stronger showing. The balance of the release detoured around the competition itself. Stressing soil, it made Page One in the Arcadia Journal.

In this way public relations serves as the mouthpiece of our absurdity, our split-seriousness, and the world of as-if. The conscientious public-relations man may well be the most absurd fellow in the United States of America. This is not meant to be a reflection on him, personally. It's just the position he's in. Not some but many of my best friends are PR men. I have been one myself for quite a few years. To be absurd is not necessarily to be ridiculous, I hope. Just the same we have a lot to answer for. The public-relations man is a merchant of what he fondly calls "images"—

little truths that never existed until he projected them from a distorted mirror. And then he believes that these truths have a life of their own, quite apart from his mirror!

I feel intellectually ridiculous even at the Crystal Palace where our PR efforts are of the most dignified sort. Here I am presenting a case, projecting an image that I couldn't care less about if I were not getting paid for it. I am a hired wordling. Anonymously, I phrase the thoughts of others. Day after day I am beating out somebody else's tune on my typewriter. I have looked at a piece of my own copy and thought unconfidently: "Well, it must be true. They printed it." The words on the page seem like those of a stranger.

Where did the public-relations man come from? Did he spring full-blown from the demands of twentieth-century business and politics? Not at all. He is a descendant, for example, of the Sophists whose craft in the fifth century B.C. enabled them "to make the worse appear the better cause," and who charged Athenians a fee for doing so. In Plato's *Protagoras* we find Socrates and his young friend, Hippocrates, on their way to the house of Callias where Protagoras, the eminent Sophist is holding court.

Socrates asks:

"Tell me, Hippocrates, as you are going to Protagoras, and will be paying your money to him, what is he to whom you are going? . . . You are going to commit your soul to the care of a man whom you call a Sophist, and yet I hardly think that you know what a Sophist is; and if not, then you don't even know to whom you are committing your soul and whether the thing to which you commit yourself be good or evil."

The boy answers:

"I certainly think that I do know. . . . I take him to be one who knows wise things."

Socrates pursues the question:

"Is not a Sophist, Hippocrates, one who deals whole-sale or retail in the food of the soul?"

Hippocrates is troubled:

"And what, Socrates, is the food of the soul?"

Socrates replies, and in this paragraph I think we may fairly replace *Sophist* with *Public Relations Man:*

"Surely, knowledge is the food of the soul; and we must take care, my friend, that the Sophist does not deceive us when he praises what he sells, like the dealers whole-sale or retail who sell the food of the body; for they praise indiscriminately all their goods, without knowing what are really beneficial or hurtful; neither do their customers know, with the exception of any trainer or physician who may happen to buy of them.

"In like manner those who carry about the wares of knowledge and make the round of the cities, and sell or retail them to any customer who is in want of them, praise them all alike; though I should not wonder, O my friend, if many of them were really ignorant of their effect upon the soul. . . ."

There is, as Socrates reminds us, a curious ignorance or innocence among many hired talkers, thinkers, and image merchants. This naïvety arises out of a number of extrava-gant assumptions, the kind that can only beguile clever men. One is that they think words can do anything—or if not words, photographs or adroit picture layouts. Secondly, they think that truths are utterly malleable, like crazy putty that can be transformed to order into blobs and pretzels at the whim of the PR wizard. Thirdly, with the best of intentions, they frequently believe that they can substitute taste for truth. (Public-relations specialists generally have an exquisite sense of taste, both good and bad.) Finally, at the base of the public-relations man's craft is the assumption that he can manipulate the thoughts of others—in short, that people are (in relation to him) stupid. If they weren't, after all, he couldn't exist.

We may concede that these assumptions have some truth in them, but there is a type of public-relations man who claims the whole pie. He makes the classic mistake of all those who don't believe in anything: he thinks that through the artful employment of words and images he can fool the people all the time—*no matter what* the actual, physical state of affairs may be.

Imagine a clever but exceptionally corrupt PR man with a house of prostitution for a client. Why, this will soon turn out to be the noblest profession of them all. Here are those generous girls serving lonely men. Their lives are easier than the lot of the average housewife! He will produce statistics to show that as a group they have six tenths of one per cent less heart trouble than housewives. He will release photos showing them happily playing volleyball in their off hours. He will arrange a press conference for one of the girls who has just returned from a world cruise. He will prove that the girls from his client's house make happier marriages than other women. He will saturate all media with these lying truths. But all the while, off-camera, broods the enduring truth, if you will, that no girl should have to go to bed with men she doesn't know. No matter how our

PR man twists and turns and "presents facts," he cannot move out of the shadow of certain enduring truths, whether they be moral or economic.

All PR men are aware of the lurking presence of these truths, and are made nervous by them, doubly so because the majority are educated people with dim or corroded memories of classic principles—which they can always summon up when they need them from Bartlett's *Familiar Quotations*. In recent years public-relations groups have sought tentatively to do something about elevating the trade to the status of a profession. (Intellectual social-climbing of this sort is not confined to PR. I have heard a real-estate broker speak of his "profession.")

A PR representative visited an editor I know and used that term to describe his craft, then cocked his head as if waiting to be challenged. "Did you ever stop to think," he said, "that St. Paul was the first PR man?" The editor expressed surprise. His caller immediately launched into an analysis of St. Paul's technique of projecting images. This fatuous performance by a half-educated public-relations hustler bordered in effrontery on the thesis set forth a number of years ago that Jesus was The Great Salesman. Both blasphemous contentions ignore the gigantic fact that Jesus and Paul *believed,* and not in a mobile truth either, while our latter-day proselytizers only believe-to-order in a client who is paying them money.

Public-relations men have also compared themselves to lawyers. This comparison is usually invoked when they take on a dubious client. In the same moral situation lawyers often liken themselves to *doctors*. The argument is that a surgeon must operate on a desperately ill criminal, regardless of the patient's worthiness. Similarly, the lawyer helps the lowest pickpocket to a fair deal in court. But the doctor and lawyer, at least theoretically, have devotions; each one has a rock of belief. For one it is humanity; for the other, justice. The public-relations man may or may not care for humanity or justice. His rock is a portable one—service.

You may be a good or bad doctor, but your reference point (whether you depart from it or not) has to do with the preservation of life. You may be a calm corporate eagle or a fifth-rate divorce fixer, but your reference point is human rights. The public-relations specialist has no such fixed point to work from. Thus, he can't even sin. How can you sin when your trade has no fixed standards?

Conscious of this, the Public Relations Society of America has attempted to set up standards of business conduct. These are helpful no doubt in weeding out many sleazy confidence men who might otherwise invade the field with blatant lies and hoaxes and dishonest practices such as ill-concealed bribery. But when is a bribe not a bribe? How do you rate sixty dollars under the table as against a case of Scotch at Christmas time? The question is not: "Who bribes?" but "What is the bribe for?" A crooked lawyer may offer a bribe to get his client off. This is a way of getting around justice, and as such (putting it stuffily) constitutes a sin. But if I give an editor a case of Scotch with the expectation that he will provide space for my client's public-relations argument, what sin can there be? I have bought sheer space. Although a principle may be involved, it is hard to put your finger on it. The *editor* may have sinned, but I haven't.

It may be argued that we now may obtain college credits in public relations. Does this not indicate a "profession" in the making? Perhaps so. Frankly, I can't imagine how the colleges concerned were able with a dignified face to include PR in the regular curriculum. A degree should be given for the pursuit of truth. Now one studies the techniques of altering the truth. If means of *altering* the truth were not taught, and the idea were to offer schooling in "information," then a course in straight journalism would do perfectly well.

Now for our public relations at the Crystal Palace. Our effort, as I have said, is dignified. In a pleasant and restrained way, we do good deeds, maintain fair policies, and politely tell the world about them. We are not avid for publicity. We hew close to the truth. Our only misrepresentations are negative. That is, we disguise certain of the company's desires, as a distinguished gentleman would hide his hunger at a party when dinner was late, or conceal his disapproval of one of the guests behind a formal smile.

Such courtesy on the part of the corporation is perhaps a form of dishonesty. But any polite person must be hypocritical to the same degree. Our job in the Public-Relations Department, as our boss, Mac Tyler, sees it, is mainly to present the Crystal Palace at all times as a gentlemanly institution, and the company as a benevolent "good citizen" wherever it does business.

Rarely do we abandon this posture. One notable exception—a glaring social error—shook our image a year ago. In one of our areas a political campaign was generating a great deal of rancor among the local population. A newsman called up headquarters to ask where the company stood. One of our PR men (it was just before lunch) said: "Well, we'll wait and see who wins, and then we'll be on their side." This, of course, was precisely the truth, but what is truth, said jesting Pilate. He did not stay for an answer. We didn't want to stay either. Our man, with the vague idea that he was talking off the record, had dropped a brick in the middle of the campaign that made headlines in every important paper in the vicinity. Both contending forces were antagonized. Our branch office called up in a rage, and demanded to know what knot-head at the palace had been responsible for *that* one.

Luckily for us, the campaign went on to hotter and more scandalous issues, and the company's brick was pretty well forgotten, although its thud remains eternally on the record. I am glad to say that our man whose truthful answer had given a false picture of the company's position was not fired. On the contrary, Mac Tyler called a meeting the following week, declared that there had been "a certain amount of confusion" in answering newspaper queries, and ordered, with impeccable regard for seniority, that all inquiries be strictly channeled to . . . the man who had made the mistake.

The Crystal Palace's relations with the public are, I believe, conducted with an irreducible minimum of imagination. The major aim of our PR program is to please top management, to please *ourselves*. Imagine a courtly gentleman in a top hat strolling down Main Street on a snowy afternoon. Mean boys, outraged by his image and delighted at the opportunity to change it, bombard him with snowballs. Amid the hail of missiles our distinguished stroller bows amiably left and right, and repeats in a loud whisper: "I am a good citizen, I am a good citizen"—and that is his public-relations campaign. In this manner we spend thousands of dollars to dress ourselves up and walk about, to assure ourselves, convey *inwardly* the image to ourselves, that our company is indeed an irreproachable citizen. Yet, I think, it is our very impeccability, the top hat of our complacency, that invites snowballs.

I have mentioned the production of our company movie— a superb example of the Crystal Palace talking to itself and calling this monologue public relations. Before even a rough scenario was prepared, a camera crew was dispatched to our operating areas and brought back what must have been seventy-five miles of film. The cameramen were nothing if not thorough. I am sure they didn't miss a close-up shot of one nut and one bolt in the entire industry. Reviewing this mélange of raw footage we saw endless parades of trucks, adding machines, meshing gears, packages moving along assembly lines, clean kitchens, clean dining halls, and everywhere, grinning at the camera, clean and happy workers. Everybody appeared unbearably happy. I longed for one frown or sullen expression. I kept peering at the close-ups of our many cafeterias to find just a speck of healthy dirt.

"God's in his heaven; all's right with the world!" sang our film. But the fact was and is that our company does a great deal of business in places where all is *not* right, where the local people are quite frequently touchy and demanding, where they are suspicious of us because of our dignified and paternal image. Why do they look askance at us? For the reason that in our public relations we do not in a strong enough way state our own self-interest. We always appear on the scene as this insufferable "good citizen." What we want is money, and in order to get it we are willing to be cooperative. That's our proper story. The locals will respect that, just as they regard with narrow eyes our pose of top-hatted benevolence.

Our department, Public Relations, is supposed to make these recalcitrant souls more friendly to us. To that end, we made the film for showing in local halls and theaters. The movie was also intended to give our far-flung employees pride in the entire Crystal Palace organization.

Under Mac Tyler's direction, we culled the best sequences from our miles of footage and put together a film fifty-five

minutes long. The result was one extended hymn to the
company's efficiency and benevolence, and most of us felt,
a terrible bore. On top of this Mac Tyler heaped a script
like a double walnut sundae smothered in marshmallows.
The ensuing sweetness was more than could be borne for
twenty minutes, let alone fifty-five. Assistant manager Jack
Reese and I did everything we could to cut down on some of
the more flagrant self-praise, but every time we wrote it out
the boss wrote it back in with an extra helping of marsh-
mallow. We were, professionally, in despair. We felt sure
that the public we were trying to relate to would hold this
fifty-five minutes against the company for the rest of its
natural life. But Mac Tyler was adamant.

The time came for a preliminary showing of the first
print, and the public-relations department gathered. At the
end our conclusion was unanimous. In the fashion of corporation employees, we told Mac Tyler ("Mac, I think it's
got real possibilities, but I wonder whether . . .") that
it wouldn't do. He listened to us impassively. We made no
headway.

Next week in the auditorium he held a showing before the
board of directors and other high personages. It was a
tense morning for him. The film had cost thousands. Now
he would be justifying this expenditure before the people
who counted. Down below in our wing of the Palace we
waited, shaking our heads over his folly.

Presently a roar of laughter came down the hall, followed
by Mac Tyler. "Oh, you geniuses!" he crowed. "Ho, ho!" It
turned out that our sweetness and light film had been an
absolute smash. At the end, as the sun died in the west and
crashing chords accompanied a long-shot fadeout of the
Crystal Palace, the president stood up and declared that it
was a great movie. The directors clapped and cheered. One

man admitted that it was the best film of any description that he had ever seen in his life. They all got up out of their seats, and down below, standing by the limousine at our front door, the black-uniformed chauffeur gazed up in wonderment as he heard from the auditorium the sounds of the Crystal Palace applauding itself.

For Mac Tyler, veteran of thirty years with the company, had known what we did not know—that in corporate public relations you begin by pleasing higher authority, and worry about the public later. So our film goes on its way boring one audience after another, and Mac Tyler goes on his way, and the directors go their way, and no one is any the wiser. How is this possible? Because there are no relations like public relations. You can go on public relating for years without having a clear idea of *what* people think of you. More often than not there is no way of proving how your corporate image is taking shape in the minds of the multitude out there beyond your ken. From Crystal Palace headquarters we shoot public-relations arrows into the air and trust that they land somewhere near the target, if we know where the target is.

Public relations is still a mystery to a great many top-management officials. Some of them consider it a waste of time and scorn the work of our department. Others, more enlightened, are aware that public relations must be considered vital, but they are not quite sure what happens next. Our group, they know, maintains relations with that powerful force for good or ill, the press. For a number of directors we have the status of zoo attendants. We are skilled in feeding and soothing dangerous animals known as newspaper reporters. These officials find us most useful in arranging wedding announcements for their daughters, or placing dignified announcements of promotions in the financial pages. Chafing under such trivial assignments, we complain that they have no understanding of our high calling. Damn it, we are arrangers of attitudes, not flunkeys carrying messages to the society page.

But the more progressive managers in the upper echelons do realize that the PR boys have an enormous task before them. They only question uneasily from time to time whether we know what we are doing. This doubt wells up when unexpected news comes in from the field that some kind of hostility toward the company has manifested itself in the form of a scathing newspaper editorial, a strike, or a protest from a civic group against company policies. Such occurrences upset our directors. They are pained by the public misunderstanding of our position. Can't PR do something about it?

On these occasions the public-relations department head trudges upstairs and goes into conference with the worried officials. Yes, it is agreed, the situation is serious and must be remedied. The cure, explains the PR specialist, is to project certain images immediately. "You know," said the president at one of these meetings, "we don't seem to be doing our job out there." The department head nods: "I couldn't agree more. We have been remiss; there's no question about that." He is disturbed, but by no means afraid of losing his job. He well knows that if we should project the Crystal Palace in the image of a mechanical monster he would still retain his position, in accordance with the palace's unshakable observance of Social Justice.

Once a year the public relations chief reports to the board of directors on (a) progress achieved in the last twelve months, and (b) plans for the next twelve months. He carries with him an Image Board, places it on a tripod, and proceeds from attitude to attitude, outlining for the directors the ideas that we must insert in the minds of the public. Each image, fashioned out of strips of black lettering against a white background, has been carefully pasted on the display board. One of our latest boards looked like this:

> "Image Board
> Some Major Objectives—
> Win Public Acceptance of These Ideas."

1. *We are a reputable company.*
2. *You benefit from our Capital and Know-How.*
3. *We are helping to achieve your goals.*
4. *We seek a chance to correct misconceptions.*
5. *We are a friendly organization.*
6. *We are a good employer—treat our people well.*
7. *We are socially conscious in our thinking.*
8. *We behave as a good citizen in your town.*
9. *We seek understanding and cooperation.*
10. *We are technically competent—know our job.*
11. *We believe in Freedom, Democracy, Free Enterprise.*
11. *(a) We are against Forest Fires. (No, some buffoon inserted that as a joke, and it was taken out.)*
12. *We work toward a better standard of living for all.*

Management, you may guess, is delighted by this pious homily. It all seems so marvelously clear. Who dares cast a stone at our worthy aims? My sole objection to them is that, standing by themselves in a PR presentation, they are wholly meaningless. Such slogans, which everyone will surely accept, are sieves. And they go without saying. But by saying them we feel that we have accomplished something. We have accomplished nothing.

At this point the PR chief produces another board displaying company publications that, of course, convey these images. Very good. Once more we happily chase our tails. Or rather we resemble a football team reporting on the results of the season. We tell the alumni everything but the scores. We run off the repertoire of the plays we used. We don't describe what our opponents *did* to those plays. We fail to explain how many yards, if any, they may have gained. So far as next season is concerned, we assure our listeners that we will employ the same plays and possibly invent some new ones. But we have not scouted our opponents and diagrammed *their* plays. Our football season, as reported to the directors, has taken place entirely in the clouds. And the directors nod wisely as the PR coach describes how cleanly our concepts work against thin air.

The honest way to make a public-relations report is to say: "Here is the problem in this area. This is what they think about us. Here are the obstacles one, two, three, and here are the steps (a) we have taken, and (b) we intend to take in order to overcome them. Last year we tried this, that, and that. As a result, the situation (a) hasn't changed, or (b) has either improved or deteriorated in these respects. . . ." etc.

But at the Crystal Palace we are too intent on pleasing ourselves to file reports like that. We are content to stick a feather in our hat and call it macaroni. Today our public-relations inadequacies, our lack of defensive planning against those who some day will challenge us, do not matter too much—just as our hiring practices, our nepotism, and our lock-step administrative procedures with the premium they pay on amiable mediocrity do not yet matter. But sooner or later, if all this continues, the year will come when we will pay for our complacency. By that time, of course, the men who now head our departments will long since have retired to their flower beds and world cruises.

The Crystal Palace organization at times shows little respect for the public-relations department. At a recent company-wide conference attended by field managers, the last item on the grueling two-week program was public relations. PR was allotted two hours. One hour was taken up by the movie. The second hour was marred by the collapse of the tripod that held the Image Board, and our images scattered all over the floor. In the middle of the discussion two exhausted field managers actually fell out of their chairs. The PR man hardly had time to get through a small part of his presentation when the director in charge of the session rang a bell on him. The speaker cast a somber eye on the tired faces before him, and said: "I trust that I haven't bored you with public relations." The meeting was over.

An Ashanti proverb goes: if the horse is a fool, it does not mean that the rider is a fool. That is the way I feel about public relations. I think it is an absurd horse we are riding, but say again that the PR specialists I know are for the most part extremely bright, sensitive, and highly competent individuals. And most of them are inordinately conscientious; they have a feel for life, and ideas excite them. You will find them entertaining and stimulating conversationalists. But with all our talents, most of us in public relations are *manqué,* lacking, just missing, not quite good enough, *in our own terms.*

I suspect without a hope of proving it that great numbers of us in the trade have to live with a feeling of inferiority, not in relation to others but inferiority to ourselves, what we might have been. We might have projected our own interests (if we had any), instead of anonymously promoting the interests of others. We might have put forth our own ideas, attached to our own names and faces, instead of becoming the intellectual servants of others.

Riding in a car with my friend Jim Waller, one of the

finest industrial PR representatives anywhere, I mentioned an idle conversation with some people the night before. We had been talking about who each of us would rather be if we couldn't be ourselves. I said jokingly that I would like to be the Aga Khan, because he was incredibly rich, and also a bona fide spiritual leader, and furthermore he could fill his life, if he desired, with the most beautiful women in the world.

"How about you?" I asked.

"Well," he answered thoughtfully, "I guess if I had to do it all over again, I guess I would be a public-relations man."

"Jim!" I was taken aback. "You mean spend your life writing somebody else's material?"

"Oh well, no. . . ." he said with some embarrassment. "I was only speaking in terms of realistic possibilities."

I was embarrassed too, because it is a silly game, and I knew that if he had permitted himself to indulge in it he could have come up with a fantasy as good as mine. Also, since I was earning my pay in PR and had been for quite a few years, it was hardly consistent to take a disapproving attitude toward the craft.

Even so, I was depressed by my own words. What else was our job than writing somebody else's material, thinking his thoughts more artfully or craftily than he could, putting our thoughts in his mind, and then pretending that the ideas were still ours? But they were not. Once we signed them over to him and he gave voice to them, the ideas formed in our hired minds were no longer ours. We gave away a little bit of ourselves every time we did this. A bit of self was subtracted from us. Our own personal image became blurred into the bigger image of the person or company that paid us, until gradually we disappeared into the team.

Strange is the PR man's goal of anonymity. For to be

successful he must remain anonymous. He positively aspires not to be noticed. Not a trace of his handiwork should be attributed to him. The arrangement of truths, the attractive presentation of someone else's story, must seem to "just happen" without authorship. The ringing phrases of statesmen and industrial leaders, according to the immutable truth of as-if, are theirs—despite the incidental fact that they were conceived by the wordsmith without a name who fades smiling into the background.

Of all absurd conditions, that of the ghostwriter is intellectually the most painful. We have a crazy public world in which practically no one writes his own material anymore. Many a noble image that stirs us has been concocted by a clerkish little writer in the back bench of a public-relations office. The great man ascends the platform—he calls for action! He lifts his hand to his brow and surveys the horizon; surely we are in the presence of a man of vision. The resounding phrases roll. In one superb address he proves to the world—that he can read.

One would think that he might feel slightly embarrassed to receive plaudits for lines created by a ghost. But the ego does not work that way. Speechmakers usually manage to feel that the essential ideas are theirs, and that the ghostwriter has merely dressed them up in suitable phrases. The more egotistical among them go so far as to believe that the words are theirs too, and that the writer has no more than grasped them out of the air and set them in type. This mobile truth arises from our concept of administration —that when you have administered something you have "done" it; that actual performance is but one aspect of administration and should be included in it. Thus, if an official has okayed my speech, the words I put before him exist as a little unit within the frame of his big creative act of administration, and therefore the speech—and all ideas within it—become his property.

At the Crystal Palace, it must be said, most high-ranking officials are generous in recognizing the ghostwriter's role, and they almost always thank him for his contribution. Nevertheless, the speech is bound and distributed in the official's name; he is the one who receives congratulations and favorable notice in the press. To be fair, it should also be pointed out that there is a Crystal Palace way of thinking on every subject, followed by the president and the ghostwriter alike. Neither of them singly has created a policy. Their mental reflexes orient them toward established policy. The ghost serves chiefly as a decorator for company thoughts, and cannot honestly pretend that he has been an original thinker. Words are minor tools in industry, and the PR man should remember that talk is cheap.

To touch again on the most curious aspect of public relations: the PR man, in a passionate manner, promotes causes which he has cared nothing about until the day he accepted the account. And the cause that occupies his attention today will promptly be forgotten the moment he parts company with the client. This produces the weird if now commonplace phenomenon of enormously worthy and compassionate endeavors being advanced by professionals who don't really give a rap about them. The copy full of heart, the messages of decency, the appeals to our civic responsibility, the beckoning to our better natures, all come from the PR man doing his job for a fee. Nine times out of ten, of course, he does a better job than someone who really cares. The person who feels deeply (as opposed to a functional put-on deep feeling) may not be so good at the proper arrangement of truth. He lacks judgment. He lacks a basic indifference.

I was once employed by a public-relations firm that concerned itself with traffic safety. Every year we promoted
what might have been called The Children's Crusade. Little
children called upon motorists to drive wisely and save lives.
This is a good idea, and anyone who has been in a traffic
accident, particularly where children were involved, will
appreciate its aims. One day we and the client learned that
another outfit was trying to horn in on the traffic safety
effort. They were rumored to be launching a campaign
like ours. You would think that, if we believed in saving
lives, we would welcome plagiarism of this sort. To reduce
traffic accidents, let's all get together. But we were in fact
most resentful of the other group's intrusion on our life-
saving drive.

During The Children's Crusade I was also disturbed by
the question of whether our safety drive was doing much
good. I wondered whether—with a certain number of million cars on the road—there must not be an inevitable percentage of accidents, give or take a percentage point, unless force was applied. Probably the best way to reduce
accidents on the road is to arrest drivers and take away
their licenses. How can we begin to measure the effect of
public relations?

This question occurred to me during a mad ride through
the country side, a public-relations raid in which I and my
associates were taking photographs of mayors climbing lamp
posts and affixing signs on them like: "Drive Wisely—Respect The Children's Crusade!" It happened by coincidence
that two of the mayors were drunk (it was Saturday afternoon) and had to be hauled out of club meetings, and also
that it was raining. We boosted the mayors, wobbling, up
the slippery poles while their eyes hung out with fear and
brutally-imposed sobriety, and we gathered knots of rain-

coated children who gazed solemnly up at His Honor. We set off our flashbulbs at this melancholy scene. I remember exchanging a glance with one of the suffering mayors, and we seemed pleadingly to ask each other: "What in the world am I doing this for?"

Still, we can't reduce public relations to that level. Although it may be said that we have no real need for this young craft, it is apparently here to stay, and everyone is exposed to it. So long as we have absurdity in the world, we can always use PR techniques to cover it up. The trade is respected today, and should remain so—if it doesn't become overstuffed with its own importance.

In summary, I think that we should desist in the effort to turn public relations into a "profession." It is no such thing, and cannot be, for its purpose is to tamper with truths, not follow them. Above all, it has no reference rock of belief.

Finally, PR specialists should avoid taking themselves too seriously. In particular they should make every effort to stop thinking that public relations applies to everything. It does not.

Some time ago an attempt was made to assassinate a public figure who, when the grenades went off, was visiting a group of children. Several of the children were killed. Reading about it, a public relations man thought to himself: "That's bad public relations—trying to kill somebody when he is surrounded by kids." He read on a bit, then put down his paper. "My lord," he thought, "are you going out of your mind? The public relations of assassination, already! It's time for me to get out. I'm going to quit this racket."

And so he did.

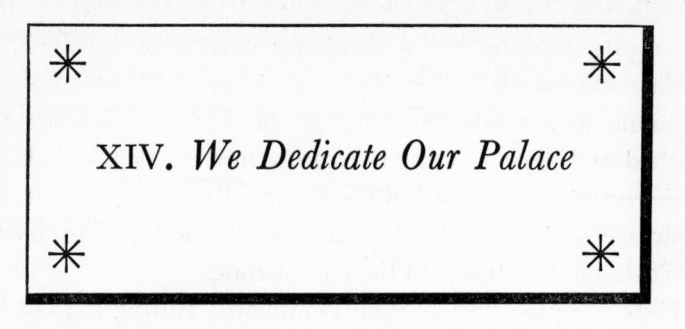

XIV. *We Dedicate Our Palace*

The rituals of enlightened capitalism are interestingly pagan. When the Crystal Palace came into being, we, the priests of public relations, took charge of two momentous affairs. The first had to do with dedicating and laying the cornerstone of our new building. The second was Open House Week during which Palace employees and their families, and our new suburban neighbors were invited to visit the institution that had arisen in their midst, come in and look around, take grand tours through the corridors, shake hands with our directors and with all of us, get to know each other, and go home.

The cornerstone-laying ceremony took place in early summer about ten months before the Palace was completed. Open House Week, more than a year later, was held in golden-brown autumn weather some weeks after the company had settled into its new home.

Both these affairs—and their counterparts, wherever they may be held—are climactic spiritual events in the life of a company. Temples and palaces are dedicated but once, and houses are only warmed once. Standing before this enormous pile of masonry, one is awed by the possibility that it may remain in one piece for a century (or at least a few decades, or anyway a year or two) after we have gone. This pile represents the coming together of millions of dollars, thousands of employees, and hundreds of laborers. It looms as a symbol of all that the company has accomplished and expresses architecturally our corporation's faith in its future. We have built a Crystal Palace to the future. Now we gather to dedicate a new shrine, and to insert our own sacred objects in the cornerstone.

Here were two special events eminently suiting the talents of our high priest, Mac Tyler. A superb organizer, he threw his staff into the production of our festivals. Public-relations matters elsewhere dwindled in importance. For months prior to the dedication and Open House Week we devoted ourselves to the home temple.

To begin with, an advance party was dispatched to the site where the shell of the Palace was rising out of the dust. We made many of these reconnaissances. At first we contented ourselves with photographs of construction progress for the *Palace Voice*. The idea was to keep solidly in the minds of our employees that we really were going to move out of the city, and that they had better hurry with their plans to buy a suburban house. As the building took shape, in the months following the cornerstone-laying, our visits had to do with the images we would project to the crowds on Opening Day.

The scene appeared unreal then, with great brown dust clouds blowing all about the site and workmen crawling through the shell of the building. Tractors and bulldozers were moving like prehistoric monsters across the ravaged hillside. It seemed impossible that the company would have a green and pleasant place here, that every day we would come to work here.

I joined Jack Reese and Win Donovan, who was Mac Tyler's deputy organizer of Open House Week, in pacing off the grand tour of the Palace that would be taken by thousands of guests. We clocked ourselves through the corridors at what we estimated would be the speed of the average visitor. The problem was to control the traffic flow and move it along, and to make sure—through the use of signs, friendly guides and other devices—that our guests would not pile up in front of any one exhibit. We stepped over wires and loose planks. The directors' floor was a shambles. Plaster shook loose from the ceiling boards and tumbled down. The workmen brushed past us: "Watch out, fellas!" We stepped aside apologetically. We coughed from the acrid particles of cement and shavings. I saw us as rather forlorn and comic figures—three public-relations men in linen suits amid a racket of hammers and saws, torches and drills, calculating our ghostly traffic flow through a building we profoundly wished would never become real.

We made our way out of there as soon as our consciences permitted, and drove back to town. "It's going to be beautiful here," Win said in a joyless tone on our way down the hill. The picture windows of the Palace were blazing through the dust. Our silent understanding was that we were headed for a drink.

We had long, lazy spring-afternoon cocktails at a roadside tavern. It was possible to lose one's misgivings in the soft lights of the bottles on the other side of the bar. "Well," said Jack, "we'll have a job to do." He was speaking of public relations, but meant, too, getting used to the crazy idea of an office building all by itself in the middle of the countryside.

The sun went down and we emerged from the tavern feeling displaced and melancholy. We stared, blinking, at the highway traffic whizzing past us and presently our car joined in the rush toward the city.

Mac Tyler, who may be the best planner of special events in the country, achieves his results by bulldogging every little detail into the ground. Every conceivable mischance is tracked down and neutralized and locked into place. We anticipate flukes that could never happen in a hundred years and lock them up too. Served well by his distrust of fortune, Mac Tyler ruled out fortune by issuing a list of Do's and Don't's to guide our efforts. A few of them were:

"—Plan to the smallest detail. Then mistakes will be merely incidents and not catastrophes.
—Use check list; then take each item and figure time necessary to accomplish work. Make up chronological schedule. . . .
—Leave extra time in event schedule. Most things take longer than planned.
—Have alternate events in mind. In case of outdoor event, be prepared in case of bad weather.
—Do not stage special event to glorify a worthless item.
—Let participants have choices wherever possible and let them pay for small items. This gives them a sense of participation rather than feeling they are being herded like cattle.
—Do not entertain too lavishly—guests may get feeling they are being bribed.
—Try to appeal to self-interest of group—not to your own self-interest.
—Do not print complete time schedules. Just give im-

portant times. Any change in schedule upsets guests
when detailed times are given.

—After event, mail something to participants such as
a souvenir or round-up book. This may cement relationship.

—If possible have dress rehearsal of event.

—If event idea seems good to you, treat it importantly
and don't be afraid to try. Most events are completely successful. All of them do some good."

Proceeding along these lines, while the construction crew
hammered away at an accelerated pace all spring, we organized a pleasing program of dedication. The mayor of the
suburb would of course be there, and county officials, and
our new congressman, Chamber of Commerce representatives, influential members of both major political parties—
and everyone should cordially bring his wife. Our field managers were summoned in, including several from our foreign
branches. Messages of congratulation were tape-recorded from
Washington; from governors of states, domestic and foreign,
and from prominent industrialists.

There would be speeches by the Crystal Palace president
and a director, and they were written. The city and suburban
press was alerted and invited. We arranged for a taped
broadcast over the suburban radio station. A film unit stood
by. We called the caterer, signed up strolling players with
an accordion, ordered two tents pitched, prayed for good
weather, hired special police to direct parking, made arrangements to huddle under the shell in case of bad weather,
saw to it (nothing more important) that the laboratory
system was under control, made host-badges with name tags
for all invited employees to wear, had signs painted and

programs printed, and ordered mementos for the guests.

These were no more than a small fraction of the arrangements we had to make, for endless details are involved in projecting the right image to the public on a special occasion of this magnitude. A phenomenal amount of work went, alone, into organizing a suitable guest list, mailing out invitations, sorting replies, and having on hand at the last moment the correct list of who was coming and who was not. And this was nothing but minimum routine. Beyond that was the creative side, and ceremony itself.

In a series of conferences the PR Department agreed that the mere troweling of mortar into the cornerstone by the company president and the mayor had little dramatic value. To dedicate a Crystal Palace you must invoke company tradition. You must also symbolize its present-day unity and drive toward a bountiful future. The ceremony at our front steps, before the half-built Palace, must gather in and hold the meaning of this day.

To symbolize our far-flung operations, we decided to mix in with the cornerstone mortar pieces of earth, rocks, and metals from the company's branch areas. There might also be added relics of interest—like a segment of a bison's hump—where an animal symbolized a region better than geological residues. Or in some instances the best-known product of an area would do.

But these deposits would have to be assembled in the mortar in an eye-catching manner. We could use an array of miniature state flags and affix them to each contribution bowl. Very good, but then what? We could have representatives from each area march up to the platform and pour their contributions into the mortar with a dignified flourish. Fine. Who now would stir the ingredients into the mortar before it went into the cornerstone? Our president? This was hardly an effective image. We cast about for an appropriate figure until someone hit on it—a little girl. Perfect. Children are irresistible, and have the sort of innocent force, the evident purity, that enhances pagan ceremonials. She would help humanize the affair. She mustn't be too old or too young. We couldn't have her making mud pies with our relics. About ten, yes. We searched out a ten-year-old girl and found just the charmer we had visualized.

My memories of the last seventy-two hours before Dedication Day are in the form of a public-relations dream, in which we ran and ran in all directions without seeming to get anywhere. Yet at Mac Tyler's command-post the details to be buttoned up vanished one by one from his list. The weather man gave us a broad smile. A row of black limousines appeared at the front door of our soon-to-be-abandoned city offices. They filled up on schedule with directors and officials, and moved out slowly toward the country. The members of the PR department fanned out on their assignments. We made our separate ways to the cornerstone.

Driving up the hill, I saw the newly pitched tents, and they gave me a happy feeling. They suggested a carnival of a more frivolous sort than the one we were going to have. Yet two hours before our show was to begin, the trappings of a celebration, even an official one, invested the scene with mild excitement.

Sound trucks had arrived. The cameras were mounted. Technicians were stringing wires from the microphones, and before long amid thumps and crackles came the inevitable "Testing! Testing! One, Two, Three, Four!" On the speakers' platform there was Phil Jester, like a great motherly bear, setting the table with bright little flags. The caterers moved big aluminum pots under the tents. Echoes of jangling silverware filled our sunny morning. I saw Mac Tyler stomping through the dust. He was headed toward a parking-lot attendant who now advanced respectfully to meet him.

Testing! That was our job now. With unrelenting efficiency the PR department combed the area for recalcitrant details. We pushed the parking arrows to make sure that they would not fall over; we tested the washrooms, checked the metals and rocks from the provinces, called up the little girl's mother to make certain that our mistress of ceremonies was in good health, briefed the camera crew, alerted the radio men, reminded everyone of the proper way to greet and seat mayors and members of congress, and finally we put on our badges and waited, in perfect order, for the guest cars to begin moving up the hill.

They came, slowly at first and then with a rush, the public, dignitaries, citizens, the ladies with flower hats, the good people coming to see a new thing. They arrived alone, in twos and threes, some in family groups with awkward sons and daughters who looked about them, bored and dull-eyed, at the grown-up festivity to which they had been summoned. But the adults were happy and smiling, and so were we to have them with us. We moved out and shook hands, and conducted them to their chairs. We assisted the old gentleman with two canes. An old lady needed a cushioned chair, and we had it. We passed out new pencils and balloons to a few dangerous children.

There were the ruddy faces of our dirctors amid the crowds. They stood with their hands clasped behind them and talked with open, genuine friendliness to everyone— not just to the mayor and county officials or the congressman, but to everyone. The atmosphere of good will that we had created could be laughed away by no one but a compulsive cynic. No reasonable person could deny our friendliness.

In the background, like all anonymous attendants at all ceremonies, the public-relations staff scurried about our makeshift amphitheater with elbow-plucking, whispered instructions for one another.

Now our president mounted the stage and smilingly acknowledged a small but friendly round of applause. A charming silver-haired man, he welcomed his audience to our premises. He explained how happy the company was to be located in the suburbs. We felt already, if it was not presumptuous to say so, that we were neighbors and citizens of the community. The company would seek at all times to be a good neighbor. As for the work that had gone into building the Crystal Palace itself, it could never have been accomplished without the cooperation of the mayor. He paid tribute to the fine suburban labor force without which . . . (and which, he did not say, had infuriated our management by dragging out the job several extra months). In short, he said exactly, precisely, inevitably what company presidents always say on these occasions to pillars of the community and their ladies. Listening to him from my position of alertness under the tent, I was suddenly reminded of a trick that a speaker had played on members of our squadron while we were training in the Army Air Force.

We had assembled to hear this man talk, I think, on the art of using your head. He pointed out that if you don't keep alert all the time you can easily be led into foolish mistakes. Of course, discipline was all-important too. Soldiers must learn to obey instantly. He would perform an experiment to check our reaction times. "Everybody!" he shouted, "turn around and shake hands with the man behind you!" As one we whipped about with one hand extended to empty air and . . . after a moment of stunned foolishness a roar of laughter shook the building.

wondered since what on earth she thought of this amazing morning when hundreds of grownups sat around in tents and applauded her for pouring funny-looking stones into a bowl. There followed the only awkwardness of the day. Our president and the mayor stood before the coffer full of relics more or less with egg on their faces and nothing happened. I stole a glance at Mac Tyler a few seats away. He stirred in his chair and half-looked about him. It was the one time during the ceremony that his face changed expression. Presently a construction worker came forward with trowel and mortar and mucked around all the material in the bowl. The loudspeaker, slightly delayed, burst forth with the good-luck telegrams and taped messages of congratulation from everywhere.

Soon the mess of culture and geology was ready to be put into the stone. The cameras turned, and the deed was done. A brief anticlimax was saved by applause started up by the public-relations department. The president bade everyone join us in a picnic, and the strolling players with accordion opened up with "You Are My Sunshine."

I had all at once a sense of *déjà vu*—that I had been here or somewhere at this ceremony many times before. It was all so familiar, the microphone-testing, floral pieces, dignitaries and their cared-for ladies, caterers, picnic with paper plates, mutual congratulations, trowel and putty. It was incorporated in a thousand newsreels, remembered without sound, of ship-launchings, and ribbon-cuttings across the doorways of new buildings, the crowds just sitting there, and on silent film run through in laboratories the speakers like agitated ducks, the courtesy, friendliness, and duck-billed platitudes of a society acclaiming itself. And why not? No reason for a vagrant public-relations man to deny the princes of the Crystal Palace an hour of pride and joy.

But, I thought in exasperation as I made for the refreshment table, we're just *talking to ourselves*. Did no one else imagine beyond the hills the presence of lean and hard barbarians who might invade our premises and take them away—Crystal Palace and all? How soft were our ceremonies! If we didn't put some muscle into our soft ways . . . those others could go through us like butter through a tin horn.

In this mood, holding a paper plate filled with ham and potato salad, I came across one of our foreign employees whom I admired. During the war he had been a partisan and fought, and had been wounded, in the struggle to overthrow those who had occupied his country. He had spent years in the wilderness and slept on the ground, had known the jagged edges of life, had suffered and lived fully. He too carried a plateful of ham and potato salad, and I said to him in an ironical tone: "What do you think of all this?"

He replied that it was a wonderful and moving event. He congratulated me as a member of the public-relations staff for organizing such a magnificent affair. "You . . ." I said, "think so?" Yes, he did. It was a splendid thing for the company to do, he thought, "because it gives all of us a feeling of belonging."

I moved away from him in an increasingly bewildered state. Was this what all the lean and hungry partisans of the world had been fighting for—the chance to belong to a Crystal Palace? If so, the chronic doubter was in a ridiculous position, and this at last must be the Good Society.

We were overrun during Open House Week not by barbarians but by friends, neighbors, suburbanites of every description, and the families of our own employees. It was an exhausting five days. Day and night the Crystal Palace was a-swarm with these various publics. Once again Mac

Tyler's leave-nothing-to-the-imagination technique paid off. Our reconnaissance tours enabled us to gauge the traffic flow nearly to perfection, and the masses of guests moved along the prescribed route through the Palace (not like cattle) as if guided by invisible shepherds.

Not that we didn't have guides. They were at every corner, smiling young men and women instantly at the visitor's service. But except for a difficult stretch along the roof where the re-entry door might be missed, the guests could hardly have taken a misstep. Big red arrows dictated everyone's progress from floor to floor. Our aim was to show off the Palace itself and to dramatize our operations, the kind of work that was coordinated by the headquarters group. At a number of points we had exhibits attended by specialists and also by squawk boxes.

The last device I do not recommend, although in our planning sessions it had seemed an exciting and ultra-modern idea. What we did was to tape-record spiels explaining the exhibits. Then we placed them in small, robot-headed speakers resembling parking meters. When a cluster of guests arrived, for example, in front of a chemical display, the attendant pressed a button. The startled visitors heard a "Welcome, good neighbors, to the research wing of the Crystal Palace. Here is where our research administrators coordinate. . . ." etc. As a PR inspector of how things were going, I saw time and again that members of the public become embarrassed when they are addressed cordially by a robot. As soon as the spiel begins the public withdraws several yards into the middle of the room and pretends not to notice the voice. I would suggest, too, that attendants be relieved after they have heard the same message seventy-five times. Perfectly normal employees begged me to get them away from the sound of the cheerful robot, and two actually had tears in their eyes.

Visitors were given a chance to walk through the directors' conference room, enjoy its fabulous walnut-paneling and run their hands over the enormous conference table, a shining oval of mahogany, across which our leaders reached their decisions. Moving downstairs by easy stages they arrived at our feature exhibit, a demonstration of the pneumatic tube system. Here they gazed at a board of moving lights that revealed the location of every tube carrier in the building. Guests were asked to write themselves messages. The slip of paper was placed in the torpedo. Torpedo was inserted in tube; operator dialed his home station number. The carrier made a swift circuit within the Palace walls and thumped home—"there's your message, sir"—in less than a minute.

In this fashion we entertained and befriended all who came to our housewarming. Open House Week was an eating and drinking affair, the only time that drinks have ever been (officially) served at the palace. Drinking more than anybody else, the Public-Relations-Department team brought the ceremonies to a close without serious mishap. One neighboring industrialist's hat was lost for an hour; a local bravo drove his car across the back lawn leaving tracks that were visible a year later, and an unidentified guest who had lost his way was found by a watchman at midnight weeping in the board of directors' room hours after everyone was supposed to have gone home. Otherwise not one untoward incident took place, at least before the public.

Stragglers leaving the scene a few minutes before ten o'clock might have glimpsed a tableau through the chinks in the curtain that the public-relations team had drawn across the Terrace Floor dining room. Drawn up in a semi-circle with mops and brooms at attention was a sloppy but uniformed brigade of the caterer's clean-up detail. Its members had been summoned from the kitchen and the corners of the dining room by Mac Tyler. A watcher might have thought he was reviewing these weary troops or haranguing them, but in fact he was rocking slowly on his heels before them, and saying: "Your good group! Your good crew! Now on behalf of—well, howsomever, it is my privilege to convey management's appreciation for your fine efforts to make our occasion a smash hit, which it was! Right?"

He wheeled toward the rest of us.

"Right, Mac!"

"Absolutely!"

"So therefore," went on Mac Tyler, returning to the members of the clean-up brigade, who were regarding him with astonishment, "I want evybody, I say to evybody, have a drink on me—and don't spare the horses!"

We celebrated for another hour. Speeches were made in praise of Mac Tyler, and each time he replied, praising the group without whose cooperation nothing could have been accomplished. Then we drifted across the black parking lot and stumbled to the automobiles.

The woodlands were dark and silent. Not a light could be seen anywhere but that given off by our hilltop Palace glowing under the stars in all its crystalline splendor. In my imagination I saw a thousand shapes stealing up the hillside —the barbarians again. How easily our limestone-and-glass fortress could be stormed over the brow of the hill. Despite its comforts it seemed in a perilously exposed position.

Suppose the barbarians had been reconnoitering there, and had viewed through binoculars the soft revelries within our walls, what would they have felt about us? Contempt?

Or might they have felt a sudden desire to press their noses against the panes of our picture windows? Perhaps like my partisan friend at the cornerstone ceremony the hard legions aspire some day to be soft. He had loved everything about the Crystal Palace. It gave him, he had said, a feeling of belonging.

But these speculations were unimportant. The main thing was that we had scored a famous public-relations victory. We had established ourselves firmly in the community. Now we knew exactly where we were. This reminded me of a joke.

Some balloonists were lost over the countryside. They descended, floating over some farmers. One of the balloonists leaned out with a megaphone, made signals to the farmers, and bellowed: "Where are we?" The reply came back: "You? You're in a balloon!"

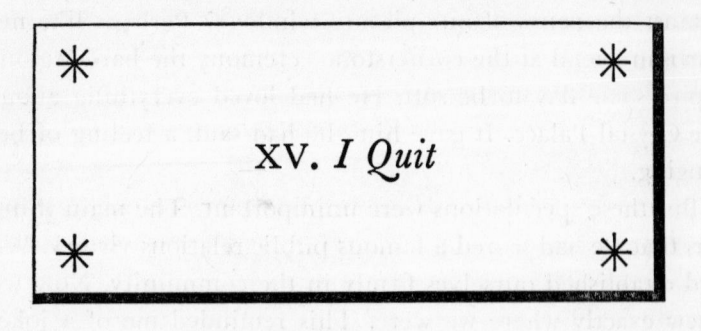

XV. *I Quit*

After more than three years with the company, I decided to leave the Crystal Palace. There was nothing particularly new in this. I had made the grand decision hundreds of times, and so do a great many corporation men. Our reasons for wanting to leave are an old story. We incomplete rebels feel trapped in a labyrinth of benevolence. We feel that somehow we are not fulfilling ourselves. The labyrinth is comfortable, with a row of easy chairs along the way. Music by Muzak comes out of the walls. Every year a gong rings and we advance one stage more toward retirement. Within the maze, accepting the maze, we are never in doubt which way to turn. Clearly defined arrows mark the corporate route that has been laid out for us by our superiors and by the Executive Development Committee. One has only to follow the arrows and trust to the company that what lies around the corner will be rewarding.

But these pleasing corridors are still a labyrinth in that each of us cannot find *his own* way. We can't see around corners. The arrows are company arrows, the soft chairs are company chairs, the music is company music. From time to time as we move along we come upon ticker-tape machines that reveal to us the impressive evidence of our net worth—

in the form of savings, stock holdings, and paid-up life insurance. En route we also encounter wayside zombies who have gone as far as they can go, performing the same duties over and over again. On each prematurely old face there is a patient smile. We salute them hurriedly and move on. Somewhere ahead is the room where we will come to a stop, the place without arrows where each of us meets his blank wall.

Yet the Crystal Palace labyrinth may by no stretch of the imagination be considered a prison. We see Exit signs everywhere. At any time we may open a door and leave. No barriers will be placed in our way. Are you unhappy? Just wash up, collect your savings in a lump sum, and say good-by.

Timorously the incomplete rebel thinks the matter over. He reviews his lost dreams. He vaguely regrets that he has not become the man he hoped to be. He thinks wistfully of what a pleasure it would be some day to make a decision on his own. He senses, especially if he has not progressed beyond the middle ranks, that a loss of manhood is involved here. True, he will not be blamed for it. Everyone is perfectly satisfied with him. Still, in his semi-rebellious heart he knows that he is no longer a self-directed man, and that he has abdicated a free man's estate. For he has a choice, and dares not leave the Crystal Palace.

A corporate public-relations man nods wisely to me in the press club. With an easy shrug of his shoulders, he advises: "Forget it. I felt the same way for a while, but after three years you're hooked. Believe me."

I am looking at an advertisement in a national magazine. It pictures an earnest and rather neurotic-looking young man of about twenty-seven in his shirt sleeves. He sits at his desk before a pile of bills. In front of him is a book titled: *Household Budget & Expenses*. Behind his left shoulder is an artist's balloon which shows the young man's wife shoveling food into an enormously fat baby while another little one looks on. The fledgling husband's collar has been torn open; his tie is loose. Clearly he is worried, and in the head-line this young American cries out: "I Want Security— Right Now!"

Such a young man, it seems to me, ought to be ashamed of himself. But perhaps he is sick—afflicted with a strange new illness that attacks mainly the young. It is a degeneration of nerve, a polio of the spirit. "Security—Right Now." At the age of twenty-seven? Fabulous. He must think that old age is an awful thing, which it can be, but have you noticed that the old men are the bold men nowadays? Cranky octogenari-ans speak their minds, and their naïve originality makes us smile.

I remember a great old man, the art connoisseur J. B. Neumann, in the neighborhood of seventy, speaking out to a young audience at a party, and telling them passionately: "People save money against sickness, and already they are made sick by saving the money! . . . We already have as much fear as we can carry! What are we afraid of? Say to yourself: 'Nothing must be,' and then you can live."

Words from an old man—the young smile and regard him coolly. But I am boring our twenty-seven-year-old friend who wants security now. All he asks is: "Kindly take me to your Crystal Palace." Very well then, take my hand and I'll conduct you there. But don't pay too much attention to what I say, because I have made up my mind to leave. Yes, really.

The Crystal Palace's new Suggestion Box program had something to do with my decision. Most companies have pro-grams of this kind. Perhaps because we were a headquarters unit—not a plant or laboratory—we were late in the game. The sound theory behind the Suggestion Box is that employees will frequently come up with workable cost-cutting ideas, means of achieving greater efficiency, etc., if they are given a proper outlet. The Suggestion Box enables them to get around stand-patters and pigeon-holers who sit astride the usual channels and react to any new thought from below as though it were a personal affront. The Suggestion Box committee pays money for the ideas accepted by the company—although the department head involved must be consulted sooner or later, and he retains the power of rejection. (The difference is that he must place his rejection on record, in the open.) Still and all, the boxes stationed at the end of the corridors serve a good purpose.

What depressed me was that, sitting down as I did with countless annoyances and frustrations buzzing around in my head, I couldn't think of any suggestions that would have a chance of being accepted. Checking over my helpful proposals, I realized that they were all aimed in one way or another at blowing up our labyrinth. I was nothing more than a non-practicing assassin. I had missed the point of our program. The idea was to improve the administrative system in its present form, not to change the form.

Since any large recommendation would be unthinkable, I confined myself to a few small ones. Not that these were thinkable either:

1. Require that all letters (and memorandums calling for a comment or reply) be answered within a certain time limit.

2. Require that action be taken on any project within a certain time limit. Or if no move has been made, administrators should explain why, and signify on what date they intend to begin acting on the matter.

. . .

3. Require that each member of a committee working
on a project be identified. Also let his specific area of
responsibility be defined. If a member of the committee
has initiated an idea or policy, name him. Also name
those who have been charged with carrying out programs. Name those who have succeeded; name those
who have failed. Do not permit the group to spread responsibility. Let the committee function in time-honored fashion as a group, but at all times cite individual
performance within the group. This may be done without editorializing. Simply say: "Smith was in charge of
this. It has been completed with the following results."
Or: "Jones was in charge of this. It has not been completed, he explains, due to . . ."

4. Establish the equivalent of the Army's Inspector General (IG) system, with proper civilian restraints and
modifications. Let an outside board of auditors (paid by
the company but not members of the company) sit in
judgment of the Crystal Palace's administrative practices. This outside board would receive copies of all major correspondence. It would evaluate performance on
the basis of correspondence and whatever other information the company chose to provide.

Members of this board would serve for a stated period
of one, two, or three years, not longer. They would have
the function of shareholders' representatives, but they
would not have a vested interest in the Palace. That is,
they would never join the company or hold shares in it.
These inspectors would report annually to management
and to shareholders on the state of our corporate administration. In addition, upon retiring the members

would file a farewell report. Their findings would be purely advisory (but on the record); they would have no power of decision.

I showed this four-point dream to a number of my colleagues who found much to approve in it. They assumed, of course, that I wasn't serious. That's right, I thought, I'm not. I brooded at my desk, a thoroughly tamed playboy. Spiritually, my net worth was zero. A corporate version of the village atheist, the incomplete Palace rebel is a cracker-barrel failure who drinks martinis instead of cider. The Exit doors opening out of our labyrinth were unlocked. Not quite, quite yet, daring to open them, I determined that the next best thing to do would be to toss a note over the wall in the hope that some passer-by might pick it up and report me.

The note took the form of an article in a magazine, the first chapter of this book, and it was called "Life in the Crystal Palace." It is not even possible to claim that the incomplete rebel initiated this, for a friend, novelist Herbert Gold, suggested to Carey McWilliams, editor of *The Nation,* who was interested in such an article, that I might write it for him.

The circumstances surrounding the publication of a magazine piece are of no great importance, I realize. They are noted here simply to indicate how a man who thinks of himself, hurrah, as an individualist, and lets it go at that for a number of years, can shilly-shally and rationalize when he is faced with a small, very small challenge. True, few of us in America write and sign articles containing critical references to our employers while we are still on the payroll—even if the company isn't identified. No one, after all, really wants to be fired unless he can afford it. On the other hand, in the past two decades people all over the world have risked immediate death in order to print newspapers and handbills.

The problem of the incomplete rebel in the United States is, therefore, schoolboyish in comparison. How can you begin to compare possibly being fired in a plentiful economy and being killed? We haven't lived through that. Since we haven't, our context is different. Our reference point, small as it may be, is that of losing one's job, and the rebel's fear of it.

Prolonged association with the Crystal Palace tends to make men sluggish and fearful of the outside. Then there are the convenient and permissible excuses not to speak up. We have obligations to wives, ex-wives, children, and all that. "Well, if I were on my own I wouldn't hesitate, but . . ." I am ashamed of the way I backed and filled for several weeks before letting the article be published.

I thought: "If you claim to be unhappy on a job, you should either get out or try to change things. Above all, if you feel like doing something about it, and you back down because of timidity, that's fine—people will understand—but thereafter don't pretend to be a free spirit, because you're not." (I also felt, naïvely as it turned out, that no one in the Crystal Palace would be reading this particular magazine anyhow.)

There was timidity, and something else—a feeling of guilt, that the writer might be doing an injury to the corporation which has always, to the best of its ability, treated him well. It may seem strange that a person can feel guilty toward a corporation, but he can. Although (rationalization again) the article would give the magazine's readers a far more favorable picture of the company than they might have anticipated, still it was inconsistent, it was perhaps disloyal, to say a word against the Crystal Palace while one was accepting its benefits. This molehill of a problem will seem

pretty stupid to most people, I am afraid, unless they have
worked for years in a palace. But I felt impotent, intellectually and morally smothered, and kept from the truth, by the
organization's decency to me.

In the small context of this adventure it was exciting to
observe the penetration of The Word into the Crystal Palace. The invasion of these few pages of print into our building could have been plotted with pins, like the movement of
troops on a military map. The printed word has such a
fascinating, runaway force behind it when it breaks loose
within closed-off surroundings. Print something that relates
to a group of people who read about their activities only in
the mealy columns of house organs like the *Palace Voice*,
and The Word runs wild. After the initial penetration all
bets are off. The outlaw pages spread like the plague.
Whether the message is good or bad, friendly or unfriendly,
if it purports to be the truth it will be read.

So far as I know one reader started it. He was curiously
enough not one of our employees. By chance he was an influential figure outside the Palace whose opinions are greatly
respected by management. He was closely associated with
the company and thought he recognized in the text a certain
resemblance. He found the article interesting, and passed it,
you might say, diagonally down to our board of directors
with a comment that was not unfavorable. Meanwhile it also
came into the possession of another executive at the Palace,
his secretary read it, and the news started on its way.

Within a few days, with the aid of duplicating machines,
copies were all over the building. The reception was so good
(from my point of view) and given with such a full heart,
that I wanted to sing above the Muzak, not only for myself
but for everybody. Friends remained friends, and were not

reluctant to pound the writer on the back and congratulate him. Dozens of people phoned, and many more, some of whom I barely knew by sight, stopped me in the corridor to say hello and thank you. One surprising older lady, whom everyone assumes to be the most orthodox of company girls, actually took me in her arms in a corner. Her eyes were flashing and she said: "Oh, Lordy, if I could be young again how differently I'd arrange my life!"

In general, the reaction to the piece was strongly favorable in the lower and middle ranks, and less and less so upward through the higher echelons. But a number of high-level executives, too, communicated to me their restrained and limited approval. In all honesty, and without vanity, I must say that there was a feeling of something like gratitude in the air. It is so easy to underestimate people and generalize about them in airy fashion, to say that they are hiding from life, and that their souls are dead. Perhaps we are hiding from life at the Crystal Palace, but I don't think we want to. I think we have been hoaxed into it, and entered, slipped without realizing what we were doing, into a boring paradise. Even so, in many of us, the lively spirit is not dead but drowsing. I know from this one small experience with an article that when the intruder comes, the itinerant newsboy with doubt for sale, we gather around him; we are excited, and interested in what he has to say. Not all the party-line mush we read in the *Palace Voice* can change that.

Also it would seem from this incident, although it can't be proved, that *something is wrong* with the way our lives are arranged at the Palace. Otherwise the reaction to a relatively obscure magazine piece would not have been as strong as it was. People don't fake an explosive response like that.

. . .

I Quit

Deep within many of us, I imagine, lies the desire to enjoy a slight martyrdom—one that does not hurt too much, and is not too permanent. Perhaps for this reason I was quite annoyed with management for not firing me. This was carrying decency and liberalism too far. I would have fired me, out of hand. But management was correct, I see now, in permitting the malcontent to go of his own accord. His position was clearly untenable. He would rightly never be trusted again, and have not the slightest reason to expect advancement. Several months later I applied for and received a writing fellowship and handed in my resignation.

XVI . *Envoie*

My last days at the Crystal Palace were sentimental. They were bittersweet. Spend three and one-half years with nice people, even if you don't like where you are, and you are sorry to leave them—though glad to go. The public-relations staff was going to give me a party. After work on my next-to-last day we would repair to the Happy Eagle, the warm dark restaurant and tavern where we occasionally sneaked off the campus for hasty cocktails and lunch.

I took a walk in the woods above the Palace, and looked down on the scene at noon. There it was, just as we had portrayed it in our brochure. Dozens of groups were strolling along the pathways like college students and professors out for an airing between classes. The great green lawns and honeysuckle bushes, the vista of hills, the nodding elms and flowering dogwood all combined to display the most beautiful seat of enlightened capitalism anywhere in the world.

I watched the strollers, and knew nearly all of them. There was pretty Janice Gill from the Library, the breezes twirling her ballet skirt, walking with plump John Bishop, the economist. Ed Royce of the Purchasing Department had paused, and with easy satisfaction he indicated to his com·

panions here, there, and all around, our newest saplings rising out of wire cages. By the time of his retirement they would probably be a foot taller. Two office boys played a game of catch by the parking lot. The ball hit the catcher's mitt with the sound of a distant gun shot.

Enclosing the oval of the back lawn was the spectacular arc of automobiles, hundreds of them in all colors, four deep. Cars like green bullets and black pearls; the Chrysler Imperial that belonged to Moses Hunt, who shined our shoes, and the four-year-old Ford of our second vice-president, Edgar Carleton. This shiny boundary of cars proved beyond reasonable doubt the degree of civilization and Social Justice we had achieved. This was the Versailles of American business, a morally justified palace, not built with the sweat of ill-paid labor but of high-paid labor, created not by means of heavy taxes but despite them.

A wave of sentiment came over me. I thought: "Is it possible to be a compulsive objector? A chronic sorehead who brays at the Good Society for the sheer stupid pleasure of it?"

In our welcoming brochure for new employees we had the president say:

"I think you will like working here. You have seen during your first days with us that our Company has done its utmost to provide a pleasant atmosphere for its employees. You will find friendly people on the job beside you, and a supervisor who will be pleased to discuss any questions you have.

"We are glad to have you with us. You are now part of the Company team. Do your job well . . . and we will do our part to make your job pleasant and rewarding."

From a high rock on the edge of the woods, watching our headquarters people strolling about the grounds in front of the Crystal Palace, I felt like the worst of soreheads. What was there to doubt in the president's message? The usual bunk and baloney? No, it was true from beginning to end, even if I was the one who had written it. Thus, the ghost-writer of truth seeks vainly to destroy his own arguments.

Still it occurred to me, soreheads don't invent themselves. There must be some reason why there is always a griper, a grouser, a hee-hawing scoffer on the scene. Possibly, without knowing it, some of us are working for an envious prince who wants to disarrange everything.

It was going to be a fine party. Mac Tyler had a good reason why he wouldn't be able to come. Instead, he poked his head in my office and said: "Say, why don't you and I have lunch together tomorrow." Tonight the mice would play.

There were behind-the-scenes conspiracies all week long, and the girls went to town to buy me presents. They are the ones who keep alive such traditions as the going-away party. Not that the men don't enjoy them too, but girls in the office preserve the memories of our trivial days. When the time comes for promotion, transfer, or good-by, they wrap these occasions in funny gifts and bright ribbons so that we will always remember them. Then the men hoist their glasses, and we all make jokes. . . .

"We're going to make you jump," chuckled George Browne as we drove in Phil Jester's car to the Happy Eagle. "Ho, ho!" responded our driver with his great hollow laugh, all the more remarkable because he was in the middle of moving his family from one house to another, and besides that had a raging toothache. But so invincibly decent was this man that he gave me a broad, delighted smile out of his palpitating jaw.

"We'll fix you."

"What do you mean, George?"

"Never mind; don't be nervous. Just a few surprises."

The staff came sidling in, concealing packages. I was put at the head of the table with Dolly Jones at my right hand. Dolly was my office girl. The sixteen years difference in our ages made no difference at the Palace. There we could maintain from Monday to Friday that sweet but half-lived relationship that so often develops in American offices between executives and specialists and the girls who help them. In the office they share a warm, kidding affection. Away from the office roof, in most instances, they rarely see one another. Tonight, by consent, Dolly sat beside me and rang a little bell for silence and supervised the dispensing of the gifts.

They had thought of a pair of roller skates so that I could, in accordance with an earlier fantasy, make my exit on the last day whirring through the Palace halls. They also remembered the childish game of rearranging Phil Jester's letter boards and gave me a set of my own to fool with. There was a beautiful photograph of the Crystal Palace. The other gifts were equally touching in a playful way, and so were the speeches and toasts.

We were all alive until ten o'clock at the Happy Eagle. We came out of ourselves, as we always do at the Palace when somebody leaves or transfers to the field. I had been to other farewell parties and they were the same. Perhaps it is because so few men leave our hilltop sanctuary. We care for the one who is leaving, and this caring lifts us out of our routine. We drink a little too much and laugh and embrace, and tears come to our eyes. We are celebrating loss. Does it take loss to make us feel this way? Perhaps so, because loss, at the very least, gives a sense of life moving.

As I sat there, this time the one about to depart with the cup of kindness overflowing and auld lang syne ringing in his ears, I felt like a deserter abandoning not a sinking Crystal Palace but friends sinking into the Middle Depths. Most of them would never have a party of this kind given for them until that day, aged sixty-five, when they approached it with fear and the stunned, goofy look of men and women going to an unknown pasture.

The prophet in his cups wanted to give each one of them a message. It wasn't very clear in his head. It concerned the *thing wrong* with our situation that had kept poking at me in the afternoon, the thing that had always evaded any logical objection that could be brought against it.

It may be that this message can only be delivered by a donkey. At any rate there were no words for it at the Happy Eagle. It was not: "Get smart." or: "Get out before it's too late!" It had something to do with "Get ego!" but wasn't quite that either. Odd thoughts tumbled around in my head, such as: "Don't let them arrange our desire!" which would have embarrassed even the bartender. Fortunately, at about this time the party broke up, and we made our way out.

There is a question asked by the Basque philosopher, Miguel de Unamumno, in *The Tragic Sense of Life* that could properly have been read aloud at our party, or better in the auditorium of the Crystal Palace—preferably during a session on employee benefits, savings, and insurance:

"All civilization addresses itself to man, to each man, to each *I*. What is that idol, call it Humanity, or call it what you like, to which all men and each individual must be sacrificed? For I sacrifice myself for my neighbors, for my fellow countrymen, for my children, and these sacrifice themselves in their turn for theirs, and theirs again for those that come after them, and so on in a never-ending series of generations. And who receives the fruit of this sacrifice?"

Next day Mac Tyler took me out for a farewell luncheon. We were nervous and awkward together. Presently two of his friends, both company department heads, came into the restaurant. He collared them and made them join us. We began playing wild poker with the numbers on dollar bills. My last day with the company dissolved in wild dollar bills, jokes and anecdotes, and rumbling laughter.

A Note about the Author

Born in Newton, Massachusetts, Alan Harrington was graduated from Harvard in 1939. During World War II he was a staff sergeant in the Air Force Weather Service, stationed in Newfoundland.

In the early postwar years he became a wire-service correspondent, covering, among other events, the first atomic-bomb test at Bikini. Between subsequent advertising and public-relations jobs he began his first novel, *The Revelations of Dr. Modesto*. Much of the book was written in Arizona, where he lived for eighteen months in a small Mexican village near Tucson. Since then he has been an editor at the Republic of Indonesia Information Office in New York and, from 1954 to 1958, on the public-relations staff at the Crystal Palace.

Early in 1958 he published an article, "Life in the Crystal Palace," describing "from the inside looking out" his experiences in corporation life and his reactions to it. The article attracted wide attention and led to a writing-fellowship award from The Fund for the Republic, enabling him to complete this book.

Mr. Harrington was recently married to the former Luba Petrova, and lives in New York City. He has an eleven-year-old son, Stephen, from his first marriage.

A Note on the Type

✳

The text of this book was set on the Linotype in a face called Baskerville, named for John Baskerville (1706-75), of Birmingham, England, who was a writing master with a special renown for cutting inscriptions in stone. About 1750 he began experimenting with punch-cutting and making typographical material, which led, in 1757, to the publication of his first work, a Virgil in royal quarto, with great primer letters, in which the types throughout had been designed by him. This was followed by his famous editions of Milton, the Bible, the Book of Common Prayer, and several Latin classic authors. His types foreshadowed what we know today as the "modern" group of type faces, and these and his printing became greatly admired. After his death Baskerville's widow sold all his punches and matrices to the *Société Philosophique, Littéraire et Typographique* (totally embodied in the person of Beaumarchais, author of *The Marriage of Figaro* and *The Barber of Seville*), which used some of the types to print the seventy volume edition, at Kehl, of Voltaire's works. After a checkered career on the Continent, where they dropped out of sight for some years, the punches and matrices finally came into the possession of the distinguished Paris type-founders, Deberny & Peignot, who, in singularly generous fashion, returned them to the Cambridge University Press in 1953.

This book was composed, printed, and bound by H. Wolff, New York. Paper manufactured by P. H. Glatfelter Co., Spring Grove, Pennsylvania. Typography and binding designs by Noel Martin.

Date Due